# From Law
# to Grace

# From Law to Grace

## by

## Simon Farris

Fourth edition
©2016 Simon Farris
Front cover photo by Arthur Hagues

ISBN: 978-15171430-8-4

# BRISTOL
# UNDERGROUND
# PRESS

# Reviews

As you read this story of the life of Simon Farris, may the Lord set you on the road to freedom in the Lord Jesus Christ. Simon has shown courage and candour in this true story which has amazed and blessed me as I read it. It is a must for people in all walks of life.

*Freddie Gallichan*
*Evangelist and Musician*

Simon is a bright shining lamp, both vulnerable and courageous; his uniqueness a reflection of the intense unpredictable creativity of God our Father, in many ways a voice crying in the wilderness, yet also a friend in the storm. Here in these pages, laying himself bare, we see into the soul of man and purposes of God.

Ben Daniels, prophet, Woodlands church, Bristol.

Simon's book has helped me to get to know him better as I've journeyed with him through the joys and heartbreaks of his early life, the trials and triumphs of school and university life, his post Uni ambitions and aspirations, to his personal encounter with the Lord Jesus Christ and a new beginning. A Cambridge 'blue' with the prospect of a rewarding legal career, Simon was once in an enviable position, but his radical change of direction brought with it the desire to be an authentic disciple of Jesus and a passion to share with others the message that had transformed his life.

How could he not share such good news? Forgiveness is at the heart of the Christian faith, and it is his faith that has enabled Simon to forgive those who've injured him and to discover the freedom that brings.

It is my hope and prayer that Simon's story will challenge and inspire others to put their trust in 'Friend who sticks closer than a brother'.

*Andy Paget, Pastor, Trinity Tabernacle, Bristol.*

Simon's story displays real reverence and understanding of the allegorical message that underpins the true meaning and purpose of Christ in our lives. His story is a truly transformational tale that defies convention and is a witness to the Father's love for His children through His grace.

*Duncan Bambridge, eschatological researcher and teacher.*

Extremely real and honest, with true feelings and emotions. An incredible journey.

*Rob White, Psychiatric Nurse*

I found this book very moving.     *Graham Paul Kendrick Songwriter, Southern Summer Records*

Simon Farris' book is simply one of the best books I have read in a long time. For someone who was bullied as a child and brought up a son who was bullied, it is one of the most insightful books I have had the pleasure to read. Also as someone who also has had mental health issues, it is a very honest and thought provoking book which needs to be read...

I have known Simon for 13 years and know him to be an honest, hardworking gentleman that would give anyone the support they needed. Also, when my son was going through one of his most difficult times in regards to school and would not talk about it, he felt Simon was the only one he could communicate with. Simon has always been a good supporter and advocate for young people and tried tirelessly to be a voice for them.

To this day I consider him to be a good friend from whom we could get good counsel if needed. I highly recommend this book which should be given to schools, colleges and mental health after care support, as it really is an amazingly truthful and very blessed book from a very thoughtful, intelligent gentleman who is being that voice that all vulnerable people need.

*Sandra Laing, Support and nursing Care worker*

I have known Simon for about six years and I can honestly say that I have not met a Christian so committed, so forthright and so zealous of good works as he in all my time within and amongst the Church. As this book shows, the Lord has worked mightily within and around him to produce a testimony capable of tearing down strongholds and setting captives free; indeed I myself am a first-hand witness to the power working within Simon having chosen to be baptised by him in 2011.

Though I am confident that the Lord will continue to work through Simon for years to come, we in the Church should be grateful for this book, which reflects the light that has shone on Simon thus far so vividly and succinctly. Given the extent of the Lord's involvement in Simon's life to date, I would not be surprised if we were to see an expanded edition in a few years time containing yet more evidence of divine love, patience and glory. Amen, Simon!

*Tom Wiltshire B.A (Hons), History.*

Jesus said, '*Therefore, I tell you, her many sins have been forgiven – as her great love has shown. But whoever has been forgiven little loves little*' (Luke 7:47).

# Dedication

First and foremost, this book is dedicated to God who has saved me and to whom I wish to bring glory, and pass on to you, the readers, knowledge of His workings in my life.

Secondly, I thank my best friend Bridget White who has encouraged and helped me throughout. We have worked together for God in everything for fourteen years, and will continue. She is a prophetess of vision, and God is blessing all we do.

I also thank my parents who have greatly supported me through the very difficult years of my mental illness, and who were put through suffering. Acknowledgement also goes to my three brothers and relatives who have helped me.

*Thank you, and God bless*
*Simon Farris*
Email: bristolundergroundchurch@yahoo.co.uk

# Introduction

The title of this book, *From Law to Grace*, has a double meaning. First, I came from being a trainee solicitor to being a gospel preacher. Secondly, as any Christian knows, we come from being condemned under the Law of Moses to being forgiven by the Grace of Jesus Christ.

This book is like a train to take you, the reader, to heaven. So get on it where it relates to you, and let it take you there.

# Chapters

# Chapter One

*Picture a young boy playing around his home with his brothers. It would be hard to imagine what was waiting for him around the corner. After an excellent education and success in his exams, there was no reason to think anything could go wrong. Having entered Cambridge University, the world was Simon's oyster. But a lot of bullying had taken place at school by pupils and a teacher.*

*Drugs played a part, but it was sexual abuse in Hawaii that led to long-time stays in mental hospitals with ECT, and a complete loss of his self worth, of all his friends, and the potential six figure career that would have followed if he had kept the job as solicitor with a top London firm.*

*After going abroad on two separate gap years out, travelling around the world, doing good work among young people, came what looked like Simon's downfall; He braved it forwards as he began to follow God, believing there was another life planned out for him – a life far removed from the one his family or friends expected, or even accepted for him. Yet with God all things are possible, and as we can see, it has now arrived. Praise God.*

*Bridget White*

## Happy Early Years

I was born in Cambridge in 1966, just round the corner from my grandparents' house. I always had a happy time there, visiting them for many years.

My grandparents on my mother's side lived in Linton, a lovely village ten miles out of Cambridge. I have great memories of their big house with established gardens on the river Cam, upstream from Cambridge, where we used to feed the ducks and geese, throwing bread from the bridge.

From the age of three I grew up in an old farmhouse smartened-up by Dad, in an idyllic place in North Somerset. It was a farm of eight acres, although it was twenty-six acres when we arrived. I am the eldest of four boys and we used to play on the lawns, in the fields and in the woods and stream.

My three brothers are younger by two, five and sixteen years.

The village itself is rather backward. It hasn't had a Post Office or shop for some thirty years now, and even the pub has recently gone. There are farms all around, mostly for cattle and sheep.

I was born in Evelyn Nursing Home in Trumpington Street. We then lived in Hitchin in a terraced house. My parents bought the house next door and let it out, so they became landlords for the first time – the beginning of a long tradition.

My first brother, Jeremy (he changed to his middle name Matthew when aged eight), was born two years later in Hitchin. We moved to The Old Courthouse in Shillington for three years.

We had an elderly cleaner we called Mrs. For years afterwards she used to send a Christmas present of one pound to be divided between us three boys – me, Jeremy and Alexander. Henry came along later.

Us four boys in our garden

My father was a surveyor, and my mother was a housewife. Mother was also born in Hitchin, while Dad is a Cockney because he was born within a mile of the bells of St Bo in London.

My maternal grandfather, Frank Austin, was a designer, making, among other items, furniture for the Queen at Windsor Castle, as well as the interior of a ship. He was a perfectionist. He bought a house in the south of France for my grandmother, where he designed the inside. We went there for many summer holidays. It is called La Mas de la Garriguette, so-called because it is on the edge of a village, on the heath.

We called it a giraffe house, as it is very tall and narrow. The building used to house silkworms. It had three rows of vines in the land, so we could enjoy picking the grapes. We also used to pick snails after a rainy night and sell them in the Saturday market for a few French franks.

Matthew, Alexander and me on the Gardon River
in France where we went happily for ten years

# Chapter Two

## Somerset

I went to three schools: Blagdon Primary, The Downs Preparatory, and Bristol Grammar.

When young, we went to the local primary school in Blagdon, which had morning Christian Assembly, thank God. We used to pray The Lord's Prayer and I remember, aged five, sitting on a rush mat at the front, believing it was 'Save us from the eagle one' – not 'evil one'! We used to sing hymns like 'We Plough the Fields and Scatter' and 'Morning Has Broken'. Great country hymns.

While at Blagdon Primary, we holidayed in Polzeath, Cornwall, where there is a large, beautiful beach known for its surfing. We started renting holiday homes, and enjoyed great family times. We built sandcastles, went for long cliff top walks, and often picked mussels for supper. We surfed on planks of wood, with no buoyancy like today's boogie boards. It was very cold, as this was before the days of wetsuits.

I can remember my mother, in fun, chasing Jeremy with a thistle when he was slow on the walks!

We went to church twice a year. Most of the pupils at Blagdon School were farmers' children. There was a school bus that went through our village. Sometimes we missed the bus and my mother had to follow it in the car, beeping for it to stop and pick us up! It was two miles to the school. We kept cows, and every morning I had to give them hay before school.

I was teased by other kids at school and called

'Flicko Farris the fairy'. This annoyed me, and I couldn't understand why they said this, although I didn't retaliate.

There was a bully called Paul at my school. One day he picked on a boy at school, and I am ashamed to say I sided with the bully. The episode only lasted a few seconds and there was no violence, only intimidation. But I felt bad about it.

Every morning I sat down to a hearty fried breakfast, with cereal and toast. I used to play with the farmers' kids after school in the fields. One day we played on a rope and I got burns all down my fingers. Mother covered them in plasters, and I was teased about the plasters at school the next day.

The bully used to sit in the back of the bus – as they always seem to. One day he became interested in a big red alley marble that I had. He offered me two pounds if I brought it in the next day. That was like a million pounds to me. I forgot about it the next morning, however, and he wasn't interested in it after that.

I remember running round in ever decreasing circles in the school yard once, until I fell over and cut my knees. I always seemed to have grazed knees and elbows, maybe because I was a fast runner and always won the races.

When it came to the time for my parents to discuss my future education, one female teacher in the village school told my parents I was too stupid to get into Bristol Grammar School where they were thinking of sending me, although I was to prove her wrong. I wonder what she would have thought if she knew I would go on to Cambridge!

We did a Nativity play one year when I was six, and I was second king. A neighbour had given my mother a crown for me to wear, but the teacher told me to swap it with another boy's crown. I tried to swap them back, but the teacher insisted we did as she told us.

My brother Alexander was born in my parents' bed. I was called in to see him in the morning. I remember how the room around him was lit up in a bright white light. It was supernatural and shone all around his clothes and his cot.

Another time when I was brought into the bedroom was when my mother told me, when I was eight, that my great-grandmother had died. I said, 'Who shot her?' This amuses my mother and must have been due to all the cowboy films I watched. Apparently, I was angry and offended that she had died.

We always had jobs to do outside, sometimes pushing wheelbarrows full of stones. This might explain why I was later able to beat the weight-lifting captain of Cambridge University in an arm-wrestling competition. We had to chop a lot of wood, and work in the fields. These were all things I enjoyed. I found it great, working outside close to Nature.

We sometimes worked all day clearing brambles and weeds until it got dark. Tired out, we could at last come in to Mother's tea. We often had big bonfires which would sometimes last until the next morning. I can remember laying cement and building walls. As the eldest, I was entrusted with all the tools, and I enjoyed scything the long grass.

When we weren't working, I would be playing in our woods by the stream, usually cowboys and Indians with

7

Matthew, making my own bows and arrows from hazel. We also used to buy penny sweets from the village shop and eat them in the woods. Those *were* idyllic days.

We visited my grandparents many times, and they were always happy occasions. We played croquet on the lawn and had family parties which we all enjoyed.

A few times, Grandpa in Cambridge and I made wooden things in his shed, and they still survive to this day. I remember reading children's books with Granny when very young. I found the books when clearing her cupboards when she moved out, and enjoyed recalling the pictures from twenty-five years before.

It was great to go to University in the town where I was born and where my grandparents lived. Dad showed me around St John's when I was eight. I thought it was special then, and was delighted to go there as an undergraduate.

(A mystery occurred many years later. Granny phoned my parents at five one morning to say she had been called by a man named Simon who sounded just like me. He said he was at a gay orgy, was in trouble and needed help. Mother immediately phoned me, to discover I was asleep in my flat in Bristol. We never solved the mystery, and the man never phoned again.)

Cambridge is a great place. You can feel the civilisation and intelligence that has been there for 700 years. I recommend to anyone visiting to go punting on the Cam along the Backs. Most of the Colleges were ecclesiastical, and I think the Backs – the old Colleges lining the river from Magdalene to Queen's – must rank as one of Man's most beautiful creations on the planet.

Granny told me that Jesus appeared to her once in

her sitting-room. That was all she said. Years later, I gave her a painting of some sweet pea flowers that I had done while in a mental hospital. Proudly, she hung it on her wall. When her house was sold, she told me the auctioneer saw the painting and got all excited. He said that it was what everyone was looking for at that time. Granny always chatted to everyone who came in.

# Chapter Three

## The Downs School

At seven years old I went to the school where I was happiest: The Downs Preparatory School in Wraxall. When I was initially shown round the school, I thought how big the senior boys were.

There is no doubt how great a Christian ethos is for the good of a human being. People were happy, discipline was excellent and the achievements of the pupils were the highest.

It was a semi-boarding school in the country, with about fifty acres of sports fields. It is in an old country house called Charlton House with outbuildings added on for classrooms. It was a left-over, I suppose, from the British Empire – we still had Tiffin (which was tea in India in the days of the Raj) and we used to sing songs about the defeat of Hitler, even though the war had been over for thirty years!

I soon settled in and made friends. Mr Perkins was a teacher whom I later came to know as an adult at church. He said that I used to talk to everyone, which is something I still do! I had a group of five friends who remained so throughout my six years there.

Morning assembly was in the hall at 8:50. We sang old Protestant hymns from the Ancient and Modern Hymnbook every morning, and had a passage from the Bible and prayers. This is a great start to the day and really builds people up.

The Head was Peter Lazarus who was a good family friend. He was a great man who built the school up from virtually nothing to one of, if not the, most prominent Prep Schools in the country at that time. He appointed me head boy in my last term, but sadly he then died in the preceding holidays.

We had grace before and after every meal, and all the food had to be eaten. There was a headmaster's table, where we all sat by rotation. When it was my turn, my least favourite pudding was on the menu. It was Manchester tart with thick, hard custard, and I hated it. Even the thought of it made me feel sick. I pushed it around my plate for the whole meal until everyone had left. At last the cleaners came and let me off. Another time, at Mr Evans' table, we had curry. I stuck my fork in and the whole lot lifted up, hanging down about a foot. Thank God, he let me off that too.

We were the best school in the country at rugby in the late '70s, winning Rosslyn Park – the National Sevens competition – four years in a row. This was, I think, mainly thanks to two excellent Welsh coaches, Mr Evans and Mr Brooks. The dads would all turn up to watch our rugby matches, and my father was a faithful attender.

There was plenty of English/Welsh rivalry on the days of the Internationals, but they taught us an unbeatable style. Mr Evans is still coaching part time, thirty-five years later.

Mr Lazarus allowed me to board in my final year at dayboy fees, as he wanted to train me up to be head boy (head boys had to be boarders). I was made a prefect in that term, and head of house the term after. These were definitely my happiest times, which must say something about how human beings like liberty. I also liked the responsibility.

We prefects were allowed to make toast, and given hot chocolate and biscuits before bed. We watched *The Secret Army* on TV the whole autumn term. We had to polish our shoes twice a week.

When I boarded, we were able to play table tennis and snooker in the evenings. There was a special version of table tennis played on the table in the hall, without a net. The game was peculiar to The Downs, a bit like the Wall Game at Eton I suppose. We would also eat tuck from our tuck boxes that we brought to school every term.

All the masters had nick-names. Mr Owen was called Scrow, Mr Brown who taught biology was called Brue, and then there was Evo and Pensk. Pensk (Mr Penny) left in 2014, receiving lots of Facebook salutations from old pupils – all positive.

Monsieur De Lataing (his real name) taught Latin to the younger pupils. And it was in one of his classes on 7th July 1977 (7-7-77) that I looked at my watch, aged ten, and made a point of remembering that day in class and noting what I was doing with my life every year on that date. I still do that, every year.

For Morning Assembly a pupil would read a passage from the Bible. One day I was practising out loud, a week before it was my turn, and a teacher overheard me and corrected my pronunciation of Nicodemus. From this, I have now worked out that my passage must have included John 3:5, about being born again, being born of water and Spirit – which happened to me when I was twenty-four.

In Assembly, Mr Lazarus had a 'persuader', a metal

comb with which he would correct boys' unkempt hair. He also used to whack kids with a block of wood for misdemeanours. There was a study list where boys would have to appear twice a week for punishment – either a detention or the whack. There was a list of green and red marks, for good and bad behaviour, recorded in the red book. When you reached three red marks you would be on the study list. Boys would line up outside Mr Lazarus' study after Morning Assembly, trembling, and we could hear them each getting the whack.

I was at The Downs School from 1974 to 1980, and it was a great school. Many pupils went on to Public Schools, although I went to Bristol Grammar School.

Peter Lazarus made a point of never entering two pupils to the same school, so they would not be competing against each other. This meant that I went to BGS without knowing anyone. My brothers were to follow later.

My best friend Simon Carter with me on Prize Day
at The Downs

# Chapter Four

## A Painful Secondary School

I joined Bristol Grammar School in 1980, at the age of thirteen. The class had formed two years earlier, when the boys were eleven, and I imagine many had also been in the lower school. So by this time the whole class knew each other well.

Almost immediately, a group of bullies started chanting the word 'phallus' at me, (meaning a model of an erect penis), as it rhymed with my surname 'Farris', I presume. Although some of them were later expelled, (they were punks and wore skin-tight jeans), the damage was done.

Every time I walked into the room they called this name out. This encouraged others in the class to join in. I now see the boys who did this as cowards, because to my face they might be friendly, but they would join in when the bullies started mocking.

This would even happen in front of teachers, but they did nothing about it. Every time I answered a question, the taunting would start. It spread to other sets too, when we shared with other classes, so it quickly spread around the school.

Not one of the teachers did anything to stop the abuse. In fact one even joined in – he taught RE. After leaving, I wrote to the head asking to talk to him about this, but received no satisfactory reply.

I was picked on and mentally abused at BGS for the full five years that I was there from aged thirteen to eighteen. Consequently I made no normal friendships in my teenage years, and only had one friend. My character was extrovert at The Downs where I was made head boy, but I was forced into introversion at BGS.

I (and later my brothers with me) travelled thirteen miles a day to reach Bristol Grammar School, but once there, the abuse continued daily. There was no letup at all. Those days were to mark my life for years to come. I got by with the help of the one friend who saw what was happening to me. For me, school was like a prison.

Bristol Grammar was in some ways the exact opposite of The Downs School. It had no spiritual identity, was in the centre of the City. There seemed to be no sense of belonging or morale. It was weak.

Anyway, I got eleven O-Levels, three A-Levels and an S-Level. BGS was a good school academically; it's just that I found the character of the place so poor.

God provided help for me when I was being mentally abused. Richard Jenkins, the captain of the rugby team, befriended me. God arranged this through a miracle. Without Richard's friendship I don't think I would have been able to bear the humiliation.

Even now, when people verbally attack me, I am still unable to defend myself, and go silent. I did not defend myself at school. How can you, if it's thirty against one?

When people are isolated as I was, studies have shown that they can turn to deviant behaviour. Studies on rats showed the excluded ones went for the marijuana that was put in the cage, for example. I went into alcohol and drugs and this was partly because I couldn't relate socially to people properly. So any readers who can relate – be set free.

I have not had justice from my secondary school. I

still feel utterly betrayed by the teachers there.

When I reported it to my old House Master a few years ago, he called the police *on me*, and I had to seek an apology from him in a police station. He refused to apologise properly, apparently because they were afraid of being sued. A friend was with me as a witness.

The isolation that this sort of bullying causes has, sadly, led to suicides. You feel humiliated because you can't make friends. These terrible bullies *must* be stopped. My MP wanted to prosecute such people. Schools must stop it happening too.

I had *no one* to tell. Even my so-called friends in the rugby team joined in.

I have often wondered how I should have dealt with this abuse. I could not, at the time, think of a way. Perhaps you, the reader, have the answer.

I would like to mention that where I have been open about other peoples' sins against me, I have never held anything against them. I do not sit in judgment or condemn. God forgives, if people come to Jesus and ask.

Another fault in schools is sex education. In my particular case, we were taught aged 14, and all they told us was about contraception. This actually put the idea of sex out of marriage into my head, which wasn't there before. It led to that and to the tragic results which I describe later.

Aged sixteen, going to Piers Dibben's Toga Party.
He was an old friend from The Downs

# Chapter Five

## Bullying

Bullying can take many forms – by words or actions. But, in any form, it is totally unacceptable. As you have seen, I was verbally bullied at school for five years, so I know how horrible and damaging it is.

Bullying can make you feel rejected and worthless. It may give you very low self-esteem and make you extremely unhappy. But I tell you, the problem is with the bullies. My friend Bridget (see the Dedication and the back cover) has prayed and counselled me over the years, and I can now see that the bullies had the problem. I have been set free from the guilt that they can put over you, when they make you believe that there is something wrong with you.

Psychiatrists say that bullies are cowards. Yes, and I say to you that if you are putting up with bullying, you are very brave and strong.

It is good not to retaliate, as this may make it worse. Anyway Jesus said not to resist an evil person. You can pray it though.

God gave me the final victory, in a way, over the bullies because He got me into Cambridge University (by a miracle) whereas they didn't get that far.

You can comfort yourself that eventually it will be over. You will move on and be gone, and they will not be there anymore. I know that if you are suffering it, it will feel like the worst thing in the world.

A word to bullies: Don't you know that you will meet God one day and have to give an explanation for all your behaviour in life? You had better stop harming another human being, and try to put things right with your victim(s).

The harm bullying can do is enormous, so a word to teachers or anyone else in authority: Step in and stop it. God will also hold you responsible if you don't.

If you know of anyone being bullied – perhaps someone at your school or neighbourhood – please support and help that person. Befriend them and tell someone in authority, including the police.

You will be doing a good thing, because many children are likely to experience some form of bullying during their school years. Teachers need to be aware of it and stop it immediately.

Not everyone will have experienced the abuse and bullying that I did at school, and I am thankful for that. And certainly not everyone will have had, or be having, a bad time at school, whether in a state school or a private school. But any school where bullying is allowed to develop until it becomes the norm, and where even the staff join in, has no place in modern society.

School years are supposed to be times where we learn social skills, and develop relationships such as being part of a group. This is denied to victims of bullying, the consequence of which can be very long and far-reaching.

Secondly, bullying creates a massive sense of isolation, and the rejection hugely damages one's self-esteem.

Teachers have a responsibility – because school is compulsory and teachers are 'agents' of the State – to ensure it does not happen. At my grammar school, never once did they try to stop it. Indeed, as I have said, one teacher even joined in the abuse, and others simply ignored it when it was happening.

Receiving bullying is extremely painful emotionally, not to mention bodily if it involves physical attacks. I know what you are going through if you are a victim of emotional bullying, and Bridget and I say this to you: please *don't* consider suicide.

If you, reading this and are a bully, you *must* stop now. Remember, those who gang up on one person are cowards.

Repent.

If you are a friend of someone being bullied, God bless you. You could be a life-saver – literally. You need to know you are playing an absolutely vital role in helping the victim.

As I have already said, without the one friend I had at grammar school, I probably would have broken. Get alongside your victim-friend. Show him or her that they are not alone. Remember, the problem is with the bully, not with *you*. God bless you.

# Chapter Six

## Christian Teaching

Youth have a void and, as we know, nature abhors a vacuum. So something must fill it. Nowadays many young people fill it with drink, drugs and sexual immorality – as I did.

The Bible commands fathers to bring their children up in Jesus' way, as many children were a generation or two ago. But the kids of today have been let down. We find chaos breaking out, as there is virtually no biblical teaching.

Life was a lot better when families went to church, and the Christian faith was taught in school. My brothers and I went to church Christmas and Easter, and to a Christian prep school, but the generation of today are robbed even of that.

I had my first moral thought when I was sixteen, and it was when I thought zoos were cruel. The teaching that I lived by as a child was to 'always tell the truth'.

When the vacuum is filled with sin, other worse things can come – I even experimented with a Ouija board – and people are looking for alternative forms of spirituality in many so-called New Age ways.

This is a widespread problem in the West. People think the problem can be solved by money. I had a top education, but there was nothing for the *soul*. People sometimes turn to cults. They get sucked in because they have no defences to protect them. Youth nowadays get their only spiritual input from music, and most of that is not good. It promotes drugs, immoral living, and worse.

The Christian Church needs to get out there and spread Christ's teaching. It is no use expecting people to come into their meetings. Christ said, 'Go into the highways and byways.' People are not going to church, so the church must go to them. Also, my friend Bridget White (see the Dedication to this book) and I have found some churches where relevant Christianity is not really taught either. What must be taught is that which reaches and impacts the listeners. They must be fed.

Nowadays, there is actually persecution for Christians like us who teach biblical values. Although youth are to blame for their own sins, undoubtedly some of the responsibility lies with parents, schools, the government, and a weak Church.

When I committed my sins when young, I honestly did not know I was doing wrong. In fact, amongst my peers, fornication (an old word meaning sex between unmarried people) was considered the highest virtue. I think this is prevalent across all social strata.

Political correctness is all very well, but what about religious correctness? After all, we must all appear before God to explain our lives. No one will be there to make excuses for us. We won't be able to hide behind man's doctrines, so let us find out what God commands and stick to that. All must appear, so that is why Bridget and I go out and teach people. At the age of twenty-four, I decided to devote my life to try and get people into heaven. To that I will hold, as does Bridget. There is no higher calling.

When I was at Law School, I wondered what to do with my life. I first looked at an Amnesty International lawyer, then a solicitor for the poor, then a doctor. But when I learnt about getting people into heaven (helping them become Christians), there was no looking back.

If you love people, you will want to do the same. Get your place in heaven, and then get others in. So the government or anyone should not hinder those of us who are trying to do this. Jesus loves us, and just think, we will live for ever with the consequences of what we have done in our few years on earth.

Please think about eternity. Christians will be rewarded for ever for every good deed we do in Christ, although the Bible clearly teaches that we don't somehow become Christians by living good lives. The new life in Christ comes first, and the good works follow. It is that way round – in spite of people thinking that they have to somehow earn enough good marks to be admitted to heaven.

Looking back now, I think one of the main verses that led me to believe and know that Jesus is God (His Son) is where He said, *'Give to him who asks'* (Matthew 5:42). I feel this is such a wonderful verse that could only come from God. I never disbelieved the message of Jesus. I believed when I first heard it.

About heaven, Jesus said you *must* get a place in heaven. Jesus said one must give up everything to follow Him, and that is indeed the case. God cannot be mocked. He will not settle for second place.

I repented, and so must you. It is the same for all of us. God has no favourites. Jesus died on the cross for us. He took the punishment for our sins. Our responsibility is to give up our sins. Sin is harmful anyway, so why would you want to live in it?

Jesus loves you, so please respond to Him. No

church or person can answer for you. It is all about your personal relationship with the Lord. Seek Him. Going to church, reading the Bible and praying are a good start, but not the full answer. Talk to Christians. There is an answer to every question. Jesus said, 'Seek and you will find.'

In my life, I repented over four long months at Law School and what happened there is the main subject of this book. It was very spiritual. I write to anyone who wants God. You may have everything as the world sees it, but are you empty and unhappy inside? Do you think about eternity? Well, there is an answer, and it is Jesus. I know this. I have experienced God, and will try to show you how you can experience Him too – in His love.

On page 108 is a prayer you can use if you want to turn to Jesus now.

My maternal relations

# Chapter Seven

## Joyful in America

I took a year off before Cambridge, and taught sailing in the USA. It was at a YMCA camp. I found it good; very wholesome and positive. I liked the Americans very much. They are enthusiastic, trusting and friendly. They loved me and would always say, 'Gee, I just love your accent.'

It was a Christian camp, and had poor kids from downtown Detroit. I was also a personal counsellor for eleven to twelve-year-olds. I had one black eleven-year-old who pulled a knife on the other kids. It turned out his father used to beat him up.

We had horseback trail riding, and just to prove how docile the horses were and how tedious it was (remember, I grew up on a farm), I rode my horse facing backwards and didn't fall off, although I have to admit the horses only walked.

It was called Storer Camps, in Michigan, set in its own woodland with a big lake in the middle.

In evenings sometimes I would go off with three other guys in a car. The Americans of that age drive from gas station to gas station buying crates of beer, and we would drink as we drove along. I was called Moosehead as it was a type of beer, and I always used to put gel in my hair. We played computer games. In a way, it was all very innocent.

We had one weekend off every fortnight and would all go to the town and eat 22-scoop ice creams each.

I slept in the same cabin as the ten children I was

looking after for the fortnight. We were asked to read stories to them. One evening we canoed across the lake and camped for the night. We would bake potatoes in a fire and roast marshmallows. The girls camped nearby with their female counsellors.

One boy, after our meal, said he wanted to go and see the girls' camp. I said no. But he disobeyed and started running in their direction. He looked back at me and ignored me, and then all the other kids followed him. Therefore, so did I. If you can't beat them, join them.

We had a good time and rolled pine needles in kitchen paper and smoked them. Not recommended. Anyway it was a good night sleeping under the stars, once back at our own camp.

I had one problem kid called Frankie. I helped him by talking and listening, and he wrote to me after he left.

On the other hand, there was a different story. One weekend a staff member held a party. He was thirty-five, whereas the rest of us were about twenty. He used to wear an open shirt at camp. At the party I was offered marijuana for the first time. I declined.

However, this guy befriended me, and later invited me to a nightclub. I sat in the front of the car, and two tart-like women got into the back. I was terrified and said nothing. He berated me for this. Anyway, when we got to the Club his trousers immediately split down the back. He exclaimed: 'Oh no, my pants have split,' and we left the club at once and started back. I was never so relieved as when I escaped and got back to my friend Emily's house.

He was fired from the Camp.

My experience was that I was a very free sailor and would give the kids a bit of excitement by deliberately capsizing the boat to teach them what to do. It was also very hot and we welcomed the swim. They loved it, and it was perfectly safe. However, the camp director, Mary, didn't like it and told me to stop. We had a Camp race and my boat won. As we sailed past the finish, for fun I threw our captain into the lake to celebrate (we had life-jackets).

Mary fumed and said if I did it again, I would immediately be sent back to England. I took notice, but a week later was out in high winds and our boat capsized by accident. I was afraid she had seen and wouldn't believe me. Thank God she didn't see. I made sure I never capsized again.

When I first arrived at Camp, I had quite a shock as the toilets were communal. I mean the bowls, not just the urinals. I sat down once and a black man came in and sat next to me and started talking. Quite a culture shock!

Then I was moved in to share a flat on camp with other staff. The other residents were all big black men. As Christians, though, they were friendly and we got along well. I remember having a massive wrestling match with one of them, and we finished as equals.

When I first arrived I felt a little insecure. I think, looking back, it was because it was a highly confident, outgoing Christian atmosphere which I had not experienced before. However, I coped.

When the director Mary disciplined me, she said I did some things well and some badly. By bad she meant the capsizing, and then she said I had spoken brilliantly to all the kids about my Christmases in England. The interesting thing is that I thought the opposite: my capsizing was genius, but I thought I had been a bit critical about some things in England in my speech.

My abiding memory is that it was a brilliant Christian camp. The ethos was great and it was one hundred percent spiritually healthy. As a Christian now, I look back and acknowledge that they had it all right. We had Bible meetings, and every morning we would raise the Flag and sing: 'Rise and shine and give God his morning glory'.

The staff really ministered to the kids and, as I have already said, the Americans are very positive, genuine and encouraging.

On a more serious note, I believe that Americans are underrated by the rest of the world. I noticed on their news channels that they really cared about the rest of the world. Christianity is definitely the answer, and there is no other.

# Chapter Eight

## Cambridge University

My father took me to Cambridge to see his College, St John's, when I was eight, and I was inspired then. When, in 1985 my University acceptance letter from Dr Linehan arrived, my father was looking over my shoulder. My eyes went straight to the word 'delighted' and I knew I was in. Dad immediately opened some champagne and we went out for dinner.

I was in all the sports teams at both The Downs and BGS, and later at St John's College, Cambridge. At Cambridge I got a blue for boxing and was elected to the Hawks' Club.

Getting into St John's really was God's doing, for I would in no way have succeeded on the strength of my seventh term exams. However, I got the highest law degree in the College and narrowly missed a first. I really enjoyed law at Cambridge – studying substantive law – that is, the substance of what the law actually is. At Law School, to be a solicitor, one just does procedure (which forms to fill in etc) and that to me was *not* at all interesting.

My entrance to Cambridge is worth telling. I had a friend called Simon Torrance who was also trying to read law at Jesus College. A few weeks before our interviews he managed to procure a Legal Aptitude Test paper from his college of five years ago. To practise, we went through and worked out most of the answers. There were ten questions. When I went to St John's and we sat before the law tutor, he produced a paper and said, 'Here is a Law Aptitude Test. It is very difficult and I don't expect you to get many right. Maybe two or three.'

Lo and behold, it was the same as the one we had prepared. I thought, *If I tell him I've seen it, I will in no way get into Cambridge, but I'm not telling a lie.* Anyway, I polished off about six correct answers and the rest is history.

I had a fantastic time there, although there was a lot of sin – an intimate relationship with a girlfriend and drinking, and a bit of drugs.

After my second year, I felt that I had done all there was to do at Cambridge, but God did his second miracle. I was travelling in Russia on an independent coach tour and there was a Cambridge couple in the group. They were both Blues – in hockey and water polo.

This gave me the idea to go for a Blue myself. A Blue is where you represent the University against Oxford in a major sport. It entitles you to wear a Blues blazer and tie. I chose Boxing, as it is weight-defined and I was only eleven stone.

At Cambridge, more respect is given to getting a Blue than academic success. We boxed for five months and the fitness trainer, who also trained the rugby team, said we were the fittest team in the University. I have rowed and played rugby a lot, and I can tell you that two minutes in the ring is far more exhausting than any other sport. I won three bouts and lost two. We fought the Army, Navy and Air Force Training Colleges. I also fought the Irish University's champion, and narrowly lost on points.

One of my colleagues said I boxed like an animal.

Well, I knocked him down – and he was three weights above me.

In the holidays, I went to the Empire gym in St Paul's, Bristol. There I fought a young black man who was only nine-and-a-half stone and I was eleven-two. In two rounds I only landed one punch and he was the only guy who ever got me into the corner. Anyway, it turned out he was the English champion for his weight!

After getting a Blue, the highest accolade is being elected to the Hawks' Club. God got me in through another miracle. Simon, my friend from BGS, knew people on the Committee. Eric, the friend I made in Russia, was also on the Committee. I was elected.

God uses these qualifications to open spiritual doors. The word 'talent' in the Bible means any opportunity. Use our talents for God, Jesus said.

Eric and Emma were Christians and befriended me. They invited me to Christians in Sport in my third year. Eric became a good friend who I saw after University ended.

I was in the top three percent in the University for my Law degree.

I have noticed in writing this book that I always seemed to get myself into disasters, but God rescued me. One example is the night I and two friends were talking to some women in the street. Suddenly I was pushed hard from behind. We turned round and there was a semi-circle of twenty-five Sheffield United football fans surrounding us. Some went for my friend Simon, who got into a fight. The other, Paul, ran off and someone shouted about me, 'Watch out, he's got a bottle!'

I had one, but I would never have used it, and hadn't

even thought about it. A police car roared round the corner at that moment. I heard later that the so-called fans had knives.

We all worked hard and played hard at Cambridge. There were lots of Black-tie Dinners, often sponsored by London companies keen to recruit us. It was all great fun. Cambridge has many Clubs and Societies and they all regularly held parties. The best are during May week, which is really in June, after the exams. Many may have heard of Cambridge garden parties and especially the May Balls.

One convention is 'crashing', when you get in without paying. I crashed a couple, one with my brother Alexander. They cost over £100 each, and all food and drink is free. With one we got over a wall, and for the other we got passes from people who had left early. Be warned, they will kick you out if they find you!

I soon had a girlfriend, and one night she said, 'There's someone I want you to meet.' She took me to a man's room and he offered me a long cigarette. I didn't know what it was, but I smoked it for a time. It turned out to be my introduction to cannabis. In my second year, my room-mate had some druggie friends, and I admit I did partake a few times with them.

We drank a lot, especially in the Rugby Club, but no one seemed to be addicted.

The social scene was almost entirely Collegiate, but in my last term I advanced to the whole University scene, which I liked. We rarely ventured out of the College into the town. Town and gown, it is called.

All one's friends for three years are within a few minutes' walking distance, and everyone congregates in the bar where there is subsidised drink. After an hour's tutorial, one's head would be reeling and you just headed for the bar.

The tutors are extremely intelligent and I learned everything from them. However, I found lectures to be useless for me, so I just made notes from the books. In each supervision, the tutor would summarize the whole topic and I copied it all down to the letter. It was this that got me my high degree.

I rowed for the First Novices VIII in my first term. Rowing is great; the feeling of unity when all eight are pulling in sync. We were runners-up in the Clare novices. My father had formed his own Gents' boat in the Cygnet's Club, and won two oars. I tried to copy this but our boat was not successful. We may have won our oar in the Bumps, but our lady cox crashed us into the bank. When mother saw *The Times* write-up, she exclaimed, 'Simon is at the bottom of the river.' My four-year-old brother Henry took this literally, but all it means is that in the boat line-up we were last.

One tutor was an MI6 recruiter, and he secretly invited three of my friends to join. He only asked scholars. One was my girlfriend, and she asked my advice. I said no. One friend, I do know, accepted.

In my last term, my mind was going. I had been knocked out in boxing in March and the alcohol was affecting me. I used to get blackouts, but would still stay standing, drinking and talking without knowing it. By the end, I found I couldn't socialize unless I was drunk.

It was a fantastic three years, a time up till then that was only surpassed by my last term as head boy at The Downs. When it ended, I felt lost. Cambridge meant far more to me than to my friends because I was born there, and used to visit my grandparents as a child, and my dad and two uncles had been students there. A friend later told me that some people used to model themselves on me, but she refused to tell me who. She didn't want it to 'go to my head'.

My hope is that people that people will 'follow' me now, as I have become an obedient Christian.

Cambridge society can be split into two. I knew half the lawyers completely, but didn't even know the names of the other half. My half all played sport, went to the bar and all the parties. The other half I never saw.

I have often wondered why this was the case, and whether it is typical of society in general.

Bridget and I returned to St John's in 2008 to a Winfield Law Society dinner where I spread the gospel and met my old tutor. Then, in 2011 we again returned with Bridget's sister Sandra, and her two nephews Aaron and Conor, which was a really good time when we looked around my old rooms.

On a holiday with Simon Torrance (a BGS and Cambridge friend) we had a succession of miracles. Once, in Nice, we had arranged to meet James, another Cambridge friend, at the train station at a certain day and time. Simon and I completely forgot. However, we just happened to be passing the station one day, and there was James sitting on the steps waiting for us. He said he had been there half an hour.

At my graduation with (from left) my Dad's mother, my parents,
my Mother's parents, and Henry, front

# Chapter Nine

## Troubles in the Southern Hemisphere

In my first year at Cambridge I was so disinterested in being a solicitor that I let slip my application for Law School. Instead, I was out partying and drinking. Consequently I had to wait a year after Cambridge for my Law School to commence.

Straight after Cambridge I secured a job in France with PGL Holidays for young people, but things were different from Storer Camps in America. I took some marijuana, and everyone got drunk every night while on site, on subsidised booze.

The sailing was great though. A friend called Liam Yardy said I should have had a Cambridge Blue for it. We lived in tents near the beach. The main troubles were the horrible flies and mosquitoes. The young people in my group were again eleven to twelve-year-olds. We taught them dingy sailing and windsurfing.

We had very healthy food. My colleagues called me 'Wash-bag' because every evening after being in the sea all day I would walk to the showers with my wash-bag. We sailed all day in the hot sun and partied all night. You don't get a hangover when you breathe fresh sea air all night.

On my day off I would walk to the village with a friend, buy a cooked chicken, salad, French bread and lots of drink, and then share it on the beach. My brother Matthew came to visit with a friend for a few days. It was a very healthy lifestyle, except that I got a few nicks on my feet and legs from the sailboards. These nicks got sand in and became worse and worse and did not heal until I arrived home. I still bear the scars. I don't know why, but this didn't happen to anyone else.

It sounds great, but it is not a life I recommend. Most of the staff did this every summer, and worked at ski resorts in the winter. It is a work-life that doesn't lead anywhere.

After the camp in France with PGL, I returned to London and found myself in a strange spiritual place. All my Cambridge friends had started their careers, and I had a free year.

I hung around Ladbroke Grove and played rugby with one friend at Bar School, and had one good Christian friend, Erik Castenskiold, who I met up with. I slept on another guy's floor and felt very much deserted, although no one was at fault; I was at a loose end.

In November I set out for Sydney, Australia, just before the Berlin Wall came down. My mother had given me £2,000 for a deposit on a flat in London for when I would start my career, but I blew it on this trip.

My first experience in Sydney was when a group of us sat down to watch The life of Brian, a satirical film about Jesus, by Monty Python. In the last scene of the crucifixion, they sang: 'always look on the bright side of life.' I saw it straight though, because of course it was a bright thing: it is the best thing that has ever happened-God procuring the salvation of people, voluntarily.

Now followed a bad time in my life. I met a few women and sadly in my first time living in a city, got lured into the club scene with drugs like mushrooms and marijuana. I also tried speed, ecstasy and LSD.

I had my first experience of God in Australia. I had a

part-time job as a waiter in a hotel in Sydney, and had a shift for the coming weekend. But I had met a woman who invited me out to her house. Preferring to be with her, I phoned the hotel and told them a lie that I had hurt my knee and couldn't come in to work.

I then got on my bicycle and cycled away. I went over a wooden bridge in a park and the front wheel slipped between two planks. I went over the handlebars and landed on my knee, hurting it.

I sought God involuntarily in my heart, and found Him way up in the heavens. I actually connected with Him and experienced Him. The Bible says, *If you seek the Lord your God, you will find Him if you seek Him with all your heart and with all your soul* (Deuteronomy 4:29).

I stayed with some relatives in Sydney for the first week. Then we looked at me getting a job and moving out. So they took me to the Job Centre at 6am. There was a huge queue of hundreds. I asked how long it would take to get to the front, and they said a few days. I thought 'Stuff that' and walked right to the front and entered the man's office. I said, 'Do you have a job for me?'

He said, 'Yes, I've just had a request for eight men in a warehouse, and you're in.'

For my accommodation, I found a hostel in the red-light district of Sydney, where all the travellers stayed: Kings Cross and Darlinghurst.

Lo and behold I bumped into a friend, Giles Ward, from my college. We agreed to share a flat with another friend of his from school, Max.

When I met Max, he was the sort of guy who made

you feel you were the most important person around, so I was delighted. However, he soon showed his other side, and became vindictive and teased me for having spots.

One of my flat-mates asked my advice about whether he should have his ear pierced. I said, 'no, as it would type-cast you as a certain type of person'. He agreed and didn't. I consider that to be one of my successes.

# Chapter Ten

## Hawaii

I had already been invited by another Cambridge friend to Maui, the second-largest of the Hawaiian Islands, and the stopover was in Samoa.

Flying in at dawn, I saw huge vegetation-covered rocks towering out of the ocean. It was very humid. I took a smaller plane to Western Samoa and then the bus to Apia, the capital of Western Samoa.

To see this primitive and poor island was an eye-opener, and it is a good place. Jesus said, 'Blessed are the poor,' and this was the first really poor place I had been to.

I saw a large ship which had been washed onto the shore by a recent hurricane, and people carried their animals with them on the bus, mostly chickens and pigs.

A man on the bus started talking and said he was the son of the chief of the village, and invited me to stay with his family. At his house we ate grey yams and I had a cold shower.

We went to the local night club where I met the whole Western Samoan rugby team. My host demanded I buy him all his drinks as payment. There was a band playing and the lead singer had eyes only for me. That just did not happen: a singer being interested in the audience.

My host warned me against the singer's interest, but I thought he was jealous and ignored him. Anyway, we all got in a taxi together and I noticed her hands: she was a man. That was the end of that!

When I walked down the street of Apia, all eyes turned on me because I was the only white man.

I had to catch the bus to the airport for my flight to Maui in Hawaii. When I arrived at the depot, there was no driver. Imagine the alarm of being in a back-of-beyond island with a scheduled flight out. If I missed it, I had no extra money to buy another ticket. So what should I do?

I offered to drive the bus myself, which they permitted me to do. On the way, a car driver tried to run me off the road and crashed into 'my' bus. So I arrived at the airport with a dented bus.

While I was waiting for my plane, the airport officials were examining the bus and I was worried they would not let me on the plane. You can imagine my relief when they did.

I saw a group at the airport talking. They were so friendly that they were like no one I had ever seen. They invited me to go with them, but I declined. I now think they were a cult. Cult experts say that if you meet some people that you think you have wanted to meet all your life, you have met a cult. *Don't join!*

I had lots of spiritual experiences on this trip. It was the start of my spiritual awakening.

Then on to Hawaii, where I stayed with my friend and her boyfriend for six weeks, working on a building site halfway up Mount Haleakala, the biggest volcano in the world, where the views were spectacular.

I didn't think that the parts of Hawaii I saw are much of a tourist area. I found it very backward in its culture, with poor beaches, despite what you might imagine. That was in Maui. Then I decided to go to Ohau on my own for a while.

I arrived in Honolulu and rented a car. Honolulu is a big city, on the beach. It was Easter Friday, and as it was a holiday I parked on a main road and slept in the car. One afternoon I went to the beach and fell asleep on the sand. Everything of value was in my bag: passport, flight ticket, money and car key. I woke up and the bag had been stolen. I saw a hotel guard and he let me use the phone.

I phoned my parents. My mother tells me that when the phone went off at 3 am her time, she knew it would be me. She answered and said, 'Is everything alright?' I burst into tears and said no. We phoned the police. The man who answered was an Hawaiian. He said, 'Go and commit a crime and get put in prison, and you will sodomised and get AIDS, or you can sleep outside a church,' and he laughed.

The guard gave me $20, and the policeman drove me to my car and opened it with a gemmy. I had a spare key hidden in the car, and immediately found a key copy shop and spent some of my $20 getting a spare cut. Thank God I did, for my original key then snapped in the lock.

I did not know how long my $20 had to last. I bought some cornflakes and milk, and then begged. I actually had the best time of my holiday then, because I was forced to talk to people. Travelling around the world solo is a very silent experience. One guy gave me a packet of cigarettes and $5. Then a group of students in a park shared their food, and a waitress in a bar gave me a slice of pizza. I told them my story each time.

My parents phoned the British Embassy but it was

in California and, being Easter, it was closed. There was a Canadian Embassy in Oahu and they got me a passport. But I had no money and no flight ticket home.

My parents eventually managed to send me £1,000 to a local bank. Mother says no one could help her until she phoned our local Bristol Barclays branch. My blessed grandmother supplied the £1,000. It took five days to reach me.

When it got to Easter Tuesday, my car was towed away, so I had to walk miles to the pound and use some of my money to get it back. The rest I spent on a flight ticket.

My new passport took two weeks to come. As I was walking to the Embassy I saw my old passport sitting on a bin full of rubbish. However, it had been cancelled. My mother still laughs, because I said I was upset because I preferred the photo in the old passport.

While in Hawaii I was seriously molested by a homosexual while under the influence of drugs. What happened, although it only lasted a couple of seconds, gave me schizophrenia. An hour later I heard voices telling me I was gay, which I knew I was not.

The illness was caused by the shock of going against my own moral code. The man had given me marijuana immediately before the incident – a mind-altering drug.

The voices – auditory hallucinations – persisted in various forms for several years until I was put on my present medicine. I also suffered from delusions, paranoia and depression. I was hiding something of which I was ashamed, and felt guilty.

When Bridget prayed for me several years later (she was the first person I told), I became free of the guilt and shame, and I am now able to talk about it, as you can see, and I am also glad to be able to use it to help others.

As I alluded to before, my sex education at school incited me towards fornication. My sex out of marriage caused me great emotional pain. God's design is that it be within the protection of marriage, which is 'unto death do us part, and to the exclusion of all others'. This also protects children from the pain and suffering of their parents parting.

In my case sadly, my sex out of marriage also led to two abortions (or rather the second miscarried just before her planned abortion). This causes me great pain. I had no say in the matter, and should not fathers have rights? I tried to save the life of the second.

Another danger is venereal disease and AIDS. I had an STD test in about 2008. I was very scared as I phoned up for the results: thankfully clear. I recommend everyone who has had sex to do this, and then remain abstinent as I have. It brings peace and assurance, and of course, is the only right thing to do if you're going to get married, as well.

Ref:   TB/RS

19 June 2013

**MONTPELIER**
HEALTH CENTRE

PARTNERS: DR K P HEARN, DR T J F MITCHELL
DR T A BAILWARD, DR R A BROWN, DR G OAKLEY
ASSOCIATES: DR A BLAKE, DR J RICE, DR S WOODWARD
DR E PATEL, DR M GUEST, DR H MIDWINTER
PRACTICE BUSINESS MANAGER: NEIL HIGGINSON

To Whom It May Concern:

Dear Sir or Madam

**Re:    Mr Simon Farris 01-Oct-1966**

This gentleman has asked me to support him in his wish to fully express himself as part of his street ministry and as a way of optimising his own mental health. He and I have discussed this including the details of how best to go about such self expression. In general I support his wish to be fully expressed and open about his experiences and have advised him that it is also important to be modest in terms of whom he directs this information towards in order not to create additional problems for himself.

Yours faithfully

Dr Tom Bailward

From my GP whom I led to Christ, and who is a good friend

# Stephen Williams MP
### Liberal Democrat Member of Parliament for Bristol West

Mr Simon Farris

Bristol

**Your reference:**

**Our reference:** BW2229/AMS
*Please quote on all correspondence*

**Date:** 24th February 2014

**Please reply to:** Constituency Office

Dear Mr Farris,

Thank you for coming to see me at my advice surgery on 21st February.

As the Minister for Communities, I am working within the coalition government to try to encourage victims of hate crimes to come forward. This is particularly relevant for male victims, who are less likely to report their experiences to the police. Although it can understandably be a very upsetting experience, it can be helpful for people who have been victims of such crimes to express themselves and talk openly about their feelings.

One of the issues I have taken up as an MP in particular is school bullying. I wrote a report which came out in early 2007 on how schools can deal with bullying. I also ran a parallel Lib Dem campaign, putting a motion through the Lib Dem conference and hosting a House of Commons reception for children's charities. I often mention bullying when I am talking to classes in Bristol's schools. You can read my thoughts about this issue on my blog.

http://stephenwilliamsmp.wordpress.com/2011/11/12/tackling-homophobic-bullying-through-education/.

I do therefore encourage you to publish your book and talk openly about your own experiences.

Yours sincerely,

**Stephen Williams MP**

**Westminster Office:**
House of Commons
London • SW1A 0AA
020 7219 8416 • ⊶ 020 7219 4802

**Online:**
stephen.williams.mp@parliament.uk
www.stephenwilliams.org.uk
www.facebook.com/stephenwilliamsmp
@swilliamsmp

**Constituency Office:**
PO Box 2500
Bristol • BS6 9AH
0117 942 3494 • ⊶ 0117 942 6925

From my MP who has also become a good friend.
In this letter he urges me to write this book and
talk openly about my own experiences.

# Chapter Eleven

## Thailand

From Hawaii, I flew back to Australia expecting my great job back at the place where I had been paid AUS $300 a week for handing out advertising leaflets for the State Bank on the street, in the sun.

Incidentally, it seems beyond a coincidence that that job was almost identical to what I do now, giving out Christian tracts on the street.

When I went to see the bank, I was told we had all been laid off.

Then I went to Thailand, as it was a stopover on the way back to England. I was there two months. At first I stayed in Khao San Road in Bangkok, which is where all the travellers stay.

There are hostels every other house, with wok cooking on the street with an open fire. It was there I got my inspiration for Thai cooking. Later, when I was at Guildford, I bought Thai cookery books and cooked Thai food every night. I still do, now and again, over twenty-four years later.

I bussed up to the North and the jungle, and went on a three-day trek where our group encountered a wild elephant, and also a tiger path. One night we were introduced to an opium doctor who invited us to smoke some, for just a few baht (Thai currency). I had five pipes, and it had no effect at all.

I stayed on the Burmese border and there were soldiers with rifles patrolling the other side of the river. The bridge crossing was a customs point, and my hostellier told me how he used to smuggle diamonds into Burma in his motorbike.

I decided to hire a motorbike and go to the Golden Triangle, which is where Thailand, Burma and Laos meet at a river. My mother had told us children never to ride a motorbike, and you will see the wisdom of following your parents' advice. I had never ridden one before and the man told me to use the foot pedal back brake, and never the front handlebar brake, otherwise the front wheel would lock.

I started down the gravel road and at about 30 mph I came to a bend. I realised I was going too fast and pulled the front brake in extremis. The wheel locked and the bike fell over. I was wearing shorts and the road was tarmac gravel. In the time that it took for the bike to fall, I got onto the upside and surfed on the bike till it halted. I have never heard of anyone doing this and I believe God's hand was with me. Imagine the mess it could have made to my leg. There were no hospitals.

I carried on and reached the Triangle, passing paddy fields. When I parked there was a very steep ravine in front of the bike and I thought, *Shall I turn round first so the bike is facing away from the slope?* One should always obey leadings or promptings in one's spirit. They are from God. But I didn't take any notice.

After looking at the river, I got back on the bike and let off the clutch. In a car, if you do it too quickly, it lurches forward. The bike did the same. The next thing I knew I was halfway down the hill. Still holding onto the bike, I somersaulted in the air and we both landed at the base of a tree. Unharmed. I dragged the bike back up and it was only slightly damaged. God's miracle.

Two bikers had been watching and were relieved to see me come back up. They were German and Dutch and we made friends. We biked together for the next three days. I think they genuinely wanted to take care of me.

Just as in Hawaii when I had my best time when all had been stolen, so I had my best time after that incident because again I was forced to talk to people. But having accidents is definitely not recommended.

Then I went down to the islands for a month, first to Khao Phang Nan. I stayed in a beach hut for £1 a night, and the food each day cost about the same. All along the 'traveller' routes were small shops selling the great literary Classics, where you could trade in ones you had read and buy more.

I had a hammock and read them in the sun, listening to ecstasy music from Sydney nightclubs on my Walkman while smoking grass.

The sea was crystal clear, with coconuts and deep soft white sand with coral. I wore Thai clothes. I decided to go to a cafe where I had a magic mushroom omelette. These aren't the small magic mushrooms like in the West, but huge.

I was soon hanging out with a group of hippies and getting along really well. They were far-out and I was told they used to fast for forty days up in their huts.

After eating the mushrooms, I went to the loo and the black specs on the wall turned into snakes and started biting me. My good trip just went bad. I came out and thought all the hippies were laughing at me. I was paranoid. This is when I thought they could see the dark secret in my heart of my homosexual abuse in Hawaii. When the dogs started barking, I thought they could see it as well, and even thought people in England could see the secret.

I went to the beach to seek some solace. Hallucinating, I suddenly thought, *I am going to see God.* I then saw my brother Henry sitting on a cloud, waving and smiling at me. He was the person I was closest to, and it brought peace to my heart.

Every month there was a full moon beach party. On the night, we assembled in the appointed place and a truck came and picked us up. We were then driven to a hidden location deep in the jungle, to a shell of a house that had been turned into a party place.

There was acid house music all night, and drugs. I recall swinging in a hammock in the early hours. It was very surreal. In the morning, we walked back along the beach in silence.

This hippie trail is directly traceable back to its beginnings in the sixties in Goa, South India, by the Beatles, especially John Lennon and his fellow musicians.

Next, I took the boat to another island, called Ko-Nang-Yuan. This is the only triangular island in the world where three hills meet in the middle, making a beach that is covered at high tide. It was truly paradisiacal. There was a restaurant where I discovered Tom-kha, the best food I have ever eaten. I introduced Tom-kha to Bridget in Bristol and we both enjoy eating it regularly.

I went snorkelling, and the coral was stunning; incredibly incandescent and beautiful colours a few inches below me. When I looked up, just dull grey rocks above the water. Only people who have seen coral will know what I mean. Suddenly, I felt a dark presence. I looked to my left and there was a Barracuda shark a few yards away. I quickly got out of the water and was okay.

I met a French guy there who became a good friend. I later visited him in Paris and he then visited me in Guildford. I smoked opiated grass, and had a hut above the beach swinging in the wind in the hot sun, still with my headphones and English Classics. My view was the open blue sea. I thought I had arrived.

One day I decided to walk around the island through thick jungle. Atop the first hill I saw a bird of prey and a perfect circle about half a mile in diameter in the ocean. Very spiritual. Further in the jungle, I came across a natural clearing and a very old tree with a trunk just like the face of an old man. I took a photo of it, but strangely it didn't come out.

I continued until I reached a massive cliff face in the jungle. Here I had no choice: I had to go back. Good job, as it would have taken me too long to get round the island in one day. I doubt whether anyone has attempted it.

One day in Haadrin, Ko-Phang-Yang, I boarded a jeep taxi, and an English woman sat next to me. I invited her for a coffee and, amazingly, she pulled out a letter from her ex, who was my old flat mate Max in Sydney. He had already told me about her and their split.

In Bangkok, I went to the mall where at a cafe a Thai man started talking. He said his daughter was going to London the next day, and did I know where she could stay? I said yes, so he said, 'She's having a party today. Would you accompany me and tell her?'

We got into a taxi and I became a bit disconcerted as

we drove miles into the suburbs. When we arrived, there were no decorations, and when I walked into the house there was only one man. He offered me a coffee, but I thought he might put drugs in it so I asked for a can of coke. It was sealed, so I drank it.

He then asked if I wanted to play Poker. I had played a lot, so I said yes. We played for chips, but he won them all. He then told me all the cards were marked and told me he was a croupier in a casino in Macau, China, and if I went there he would deal me good cards and we would split the profit. I said okay, just to get out.

He took me on his motorbike, which I didn't like as there was no escape. Thank God he took me to the main road and a taxi came by. He then asked me for money. Thai money is all low denomination notes, so I opened my wallet and gave him a bunch. I was very relieved when I got back to my hostel. A cautionary tale indeed.

I think I found (or did I lose?) myself there. I wore ethnic clothes, grew my hair, was listening to house music on my headphones, and I'm sorry to say I smoked a lot of cannabis. I enjoyed the excellent food and just relaxed. This was far removed from my forthcoming time at Guildford Law School and being a London solicitor.

When I got back to London my friends said I had changed. My mother told me I had lost my way. Whichever way, I enjoyed life, and wasn't interested in just making money. I bought a VW Beetle car for Law School and sprayed it blue and green.

England was a culture shock. Surely the poor (for Thailand was poor) know how to live better than the rich. Jesus said, 'Don't seek material riches, but rather those of heaven.' He also said that if' you do God's will, He will provide'.

There's nothing wrong with working. In fact, it is a must. It is just a matter of your motivation and priority.

Bridget rightly observed that in Thailand I neither lost nor found myself, but God found me.

I was never interested in making money. In fact, I never thought about my future at all.

In Thailand, especially on the beaches, I believe I gained an identity. I carved out a happy life- on £1 per day excellent food, and the same for my hut. I want to talk about 'living levels'. I had a very simple life, just enjoying the sun, sea and the beautiful scenery. There, I had the basics in place.

In our very complicated Western world, especially in cities where there is not much of the natural world to enjoy, and also where there are many ingredients to attend to, the lesson I learned, is that, as with building a pyramid, you have to put the basics in first, before you can put in the more subtle, and difficult, higher layers.

My family and me (2$^{nd}$ from the right). This was taken before my prayers for deliverance by Bridget. Please compare with the one on the back cover after deliverance.

# Chapter Twelve

## My Conversion at Guildford Law School

I returned from the Southern Hemisphere, very un-acclimatised to the world of earning money in London. My old friends had started their careers and I felt a bit disconcerted at having to keep up with our expensive lifestyle without a job.

In Guildford I found I was talking about religion. Again, all uncontrived and natural – obviously the Holy Spirit having worked.

My first thought was that the most healthy way to eat would be to eat locally and seasonally. For example, root vegetables in the winter give us carbohydrates, and lighter fruit is needed in the summer. This I thought was the working of God. Note: it now accords with modern environmental teaching re food miles etc.

When I arrived at Law School I thought I was very intelligent, so I bought a book called *The Glass Bead Game,* a philosophical book aimed at the high intelligentsia. I was brought down because I could only read half of it.

Next, I bought *Milan Kundera* and read it through, but became very concerned about my mind, as I could not even remember the protagonists' names. I thought this was *not* looking good for a year of Law School.

When I revised for my first term mocks, I knew something was wrong with my brain, even though I passed those exams. Things were going downhill.

When I was with my girlfriend, paranoia set in.

Although I hadn't told anyone, I still thought people could see inside my heart, and see the dirty secret of my abuse in Hawaii, even though I was no longer taking drugs.

In the spring of 1991 I guess I was seeking God without realising it. The other way of describing what was happening to me is that I was repenting. This is an action of the Holy Spirit who was acting on me without any Christian teaching. Just God and me. I gave up fornication as there was no love in it. Then I realised that I could not carry on living with paranoia, so I decided to give up all drugs. The next morning I woke up paranoia free, which I believe was a miracle.

This brought me to what I call a more 'honest natural place' which was a very spiritual place, in which I started sitting on the floor and writing poetry. I also did some painting. This, while all my peers were doing full-time law studies and nothing else. I now eat as much organic food as I can. I have learned though, that for variety, one must eat non-organic sometimes as well.

*From Law to Grace* describes God's moving of the human race from being under the condemnation of the Law of Moses, to being recipients of eternal life by the graceful gift of Jesus dying for our sins.

So although I was studying to become a solicitor, I am now a preacher of Jesus Christ. Hallelujah. It is an infinitely better career. I enjoy it immensely. I have a perfect Boss, and I *want* to do it. When you've found your vocation in life there is no looking back

At Law School I was unhappy for the first time in my life, in spite of previous experiences. I wanted a social life, and there was none. I lived on my own, in a village.

So I was seeking solutions. I was so paranoid that I was unable to talk to my mother without a couple of pints inside me.

Everything seemed to be operating against me passing Law School. For example, I was refused a parking permit for the Law School grounds. Spaces were rationed. Two friends of mine, living together, were given one each, while I, on my own, was denied one. So I had to find a place on the roads, which normally entailed climbing over a high wall every morning to get to my lectures.

Also, living on my own I had to shop, and cook every night, whereas those sharing could take it in turns. I found that after morning lectures, and an afternoon nap which I seemed to need, and cooking, it was time to go to bed. There was never any time for the homework.

I realised how blessed I had been at Cambridge where all meals were provided. It certainly enabled us to get better grades.

I took a part-time cleaning job for a while. That was a bad idea, as it stopped me studying. I fell behind in my studies and never recovered. At Cambridge I had enjoyed learning what the Law was, but training to be a solicitor was just about form-filling and so on. It was doing a job, basically, and it was not at all interesting for me.

That Christmas I was lying in bed at home as the church bells were ringing, wondering whether to go to church. Just as I thought, *Shall I go, or not?* there was a loud clap of thunder right outside the window, but no storm. I thought, *This is God saying that He exists, and He wants me to go to church.*

Later that spring I was playing football and couldn't get the ball. So I thought, *Hang on, if God is there He can get me the ball.* So I prayed, 'God, bring me the ball.' It landed at my feet at that instant. After ten minutes I thought, *I can do that again.* So I prayed. 'God, bring me the ball.' At that *instant* the ball again landed at my feet. I felt the Spirit of God hovering about twenty feet above me. I didn't dare pray it a third time.

A little later I was in my flat and decided to drive into town and buy a book on Sociology. I went into the bookshop and came home with a Bible instead, without knowing how. Obviously the Holy Spirit – in hindsight.

Anyway, I flipped the Bible open and my eyes lighted on the Scripture: 'In the last days there will be wars and rumours of wars.' That was exactly what I had been thinking about for the previous three (significant – like Jesus in the tomb) days, as it was during the First Gulf War, and I thought to myself, *This book is true.*

I got into the habit then of reading the Bible, and it brought comfort to my heart. The Bible is the Word of God. It is God speaking to us.

Guildford was and is a very spiritual place. I lived in Albury where there is an old church up a steep sandy hill on a Pilgrim trail. I went there often and one day the whole path was covered in reeds, and I realised it was Palm Sunday. Up the other side was a large wilderness, and on another day, when everyone was revising, a Cambridge friend called Richard Atherton, who was also at BGS and went to Freshfields, saw my car and came to find me. I was seeking God, getting spoken to by His workings with the sun and clouds. Richard took note of this in a positive way.

Later, when I was about to be baptised, I was wondering whether to tell my parents about it. I opened the Bible for direction, and it opened at the passage, 'Honour thy parents.' So I phoned them.

I was a diligent person who in the past had always revised hard for every exam, but this time it never even occurred to me to do it. I started writing poetry and painting while sitting on the floor. This, while I should have been revising. I got a shock when I saw my result in the Easter term mocks – only thirty-three percent! With the knowledge I have now, I believe I was filled with the Holy Ghost. I experienced personal revival and an awakening.

At Cambridge and for my O-Levels and A-Levels I always devised a short-cut system for the work, but throughout Law School I sought one in vain. With every week that passed I watched time slipping away, and the work backlog increasing, and my failure looming larger. It was frightening.

A friend told my godmother about this when they met at a church years later, that I was seen going downhill. In spite of this, no one tried to help me in any way.

In my mentally ill state, I was radically repenting. That was separate from the illness. Acts 10:4 says God responded to Cornelius' prayers and giving, and I think God witnessed my repentance, and responded. But my mind was *not* on Law; I was interested in life. I think it was Thailand that opened me up to this.

When I did finally settle down to revise, my rug got infested with fleas, so I had to spend the next week getting rid of them from the flat. I became so mentally ill that I could not even talk to my friends. We had to play word-games, as I could not cope with ordinary conversation.

I was seeing a homeopath at this time, and she had been recommending better living for body and soul, but it was my Bible that brought comfort to my soul, which was something that solicitors' studies did not manage to do. I realised the Bible is the true Word of God, and I never looked back. God had hooked me and was reeling me in.

I had got my life 'right' by searching for what to do with my life. I drew up from my memory that there were such things as Proverbs: advice on how to live. Later, one night I thought back again and remembered to pray before I went to sleep. So I prayed the Lord's Prayer, with my head on the pillow, and fell fast asleep. I did that for three nights, and then things started to happen.

I prayed for specific things, and they were granted. God was literally speaking straight to my heart through everything I read for weeks. God was communicating with me in an amazing way. Suddenly I started noticing the Christian Union advertisements, and the topic to be discussed was always specially for me from God. Also, I would open the Bible and God would speak to me, as He does today. But as I was soon to discover, this has to be done with wisdom and prayer.

I was in the habit of (partially) jumping the lunch queue at Law School, but in the time that I was really seeking God, I decided to wait my turn at the back. Then God rewarded me. The only Christian in my class came and joined the queue immediately behind me, so I was able to have my first conversation of the year with him, which I had wanted to. *And* he blessed me, into the bargain.

God works. One day I ran out of the flat, grabbed a friend's bike and cycled madly down the road to the local church, went in and found, by a beautiful window, a script saying that there is a spiritual battle going on for every human life – a battle in the heavenlies between good and evil. God and Satan. So let the people of London and elsewhere who read this, know that God, and heaven and Judgment Day, are real. So please get right with God.

This book is about coming to salvation. Repentance is a gift from God. It is an enrichment. You cannot serve God and money.

As I have already said, God used to answer me through the Bible, as He does many Christians. I would flip open the Bible and find my answer. However, there came a time when I kept getting words about being wicked. I then realised God was saying I was beginning to use His Book like witchcraft, so I stopped doing that.

God gives general and specific commands. For example, in the year 2000 Jesus commissioned me to fulltime street evangelism, which you may not be commanded to do. I have been preaching the gospel ever since, and tens of thousands have heard about the love and forgiveness of God, often for the first time, and more than a thousand of them have been saved – glory to God.

I befriended my neighbour, Richard Cobb, from the year below me at St. John's, and his 2 flatmates, and we had great times. They introduced me to playing music (not just listening), and we had spiritual times listening to Pink Floyd: The dark side of the moon, etc. We also, with a group, put on a play at Law School, Toad of Toad Hall by A.A. Milne and Kenneth Grahame. Couple this with my poetry and painting and it is clear to see I was on a different trip. I did the lighting as I didn't think my acting was up to it.

I also was very into 'my' music and used to play my acid house and house music at parties. (I mean other peoples' music, not my own). I thought of doing side-line DJ work as well, which I think a lot of young fans do.

At the beginning of the year I trained with the Rugby Club, but was instantly put off by the domination of the trainer, telling us what to do. In all my previous years, I had not noticed this sort of attitude, but I had woken up spiritually by this time. I didn't go back and preferred peace.

# Chapter Thirteen

## The London Church of Christ

Most of what follows took place while I was at Guildford Law School, where I became lonely for the first time in my life. I thought, *I can't live like this*, so I immediately decided to let out my flat and move somewhere to share a house.

When I advertised on the Law School notice board for someone to take over my flat, a man called Patrick Bernard replied. I arranged to meet him in the restaurant. When I walked in, there was this black man sitting at the table with the biggest grin you've ever seen.

He was a Christian and said he wanted to move out of his shared house because a woman there was making advances to him. This was the first man I had ever met with that attitude, and I was attracted by the Christian purity.

I drove him to my flat. As soon as he walked in, he behaved like no one I had ever met. At first, he complimented me on my Van Gogh poster I had bought at the Edinburgh Fringe, and then he asked me for a banana.

When we sat down, he saw on my desk an article from the homeopathic doctor I was corresponding with, entitled *The Secret to Health and Happiness*. He said, 'Is that what you are looking for?'

I said, 'Isn't everybody?'

He replied, 'I'm not; I'm a Christian.'

That got me thinking.

Two weeks later, Patrick phoned me, and out of the

blue asked me, 'Do you want to come to church?' I had been looking in vain for a decent church, and my heart leapt for joy. Literally. There was a physical feeling in my spiritual heart. This shows the crucial importance of Christians sharing our faith.

This was the London Church of Christ. I drove there and at the meeting the preacher spoke on Revelation 1: the glorified, risen Jesus in heaven.

A group of us from the church went to the park afterwards where we had a picnic, and I found everyone to be instantly friends. Patrick was the first black friend I had had. This was how God worked, for I was into reggae at the time. In their church in London I soon started driving Patrick and his friends around in my VW Beetle which I had sprayed blue and green.

The sun shone all summer, the windows were down, and I had reggae music blaring out with three black Christian friends in the car. A far cry from the people I had left behind while studying law. God obviously used this experience to help draw me in.

They shared Romans 6:4 with me, where Paul talks of being buried with Christ in baptism, and rising up to new life. In the church study I had been asked to fast for twenty-four hours, and the experience made me feel like I was stoned. I told the guy this and he rebuked me. I was so eager to be born again that I thought in my mentally ill state that I had to lie prostate on the floor and hold his feet. So I did, and said, 'Take me with you.'

In another Bible study, before baptism I was asked to pray. A huge battle went on within me because I thought I was only allowed to pray the Lord's Prayer literally. Lance, the leader, was really encouraging me to use my own words from my heart. Eventually, I broke free and did. He was happy. I had been stuck in a legalistic error.

Jesus said, *'Enter through the narrow gate. For wide is the gate and broad is the road that leads to destruction, and many enter through it. But small is the gate and narrow the road that leads to life, and only a few find it'* (Matthew 7:13-14).

When I first went into the home of someone from the Church of Christ, having been too afraid to enter on my first invitation, there was an Irish man called Cornelius O'Connor sitting on the sitting-room floor. 1 Corinthians 14:24-25 says that when an unbeliever comes into church, his heart will be revealed. This happened to me: I saw that I was selfish in wanting sex. I told Con this, and he pointed me to Psalm 51. I made this my personal Scripture and later read it out at my baptism. I shall give you this, as it is worth it:

> *'Have mercy on me, O God,*
> > *According to your unfailing love;*
> *Blot out my transgressions.*
> > *Wash away all my iniquity*
> *And cleanse me from my sin.*
> > *For I know my transgressions,*
> *And my sin is always before me.*
> > *Against you, you only, have I sinned,*
> *So that you are proved right when you speak*
> > *And justified when you judge.*
> *Surely I was sinful at birth,*
> > *Sinful from the time my mother conceived me.*
> *Surely you desire truth in the inner parts;*

*You teach me wisdom in the inmost place.*
*Cleanse me with hyssop, and I will be clean;*
*Wash me, and I will be whiter than snow.*
*Let me hear joy and gladness;*
*Hide your face from my sins*
*And blot out all my iniquity.*
*Create in me a pure heart, O God,*
*And renew a steadfast spirit within me…*
*Then will I teach transgressors your ways;*
*And sinners shall be converted to you.'*

In my discipleship Bible studies, five verses meant a lot to me. In Mark 1:17, when Jesus said the disciples, 'Come follow Me, and I will make you fishers of men,' the Bible says that they *immediately* left their nets and followed. This resonated with me. Our response to Jesus must be immediate.

Secondly, Jesus spoke about counting the cost of being His disciple. When this was explained to me, I thought that in comparison with receiving a place in heaven, the cost is irrelevant. Therefore, for me that was no problem. Thirdly, Jesus says, 'If anyone would come after Me, he must deny himself and take up his cross daily and follow Me.'

Next, He also said that 'If a man seeks to gain his life, he will lose it, but if he loses his life for My sake and the gospel's, he will save it.' I had already had the Great Commission (spreading the gospel) explained to me, and I caught a vision of me street evangelising, and I was willing to do it unto death. This accords with Revelation 12:11, which says, 'And they overcame him by the blood of the Lamb, and by the word of their testimony; and they loved not their lives unto the death' (KJV). So I knew, and I also now know when I often look back, that I had repented. This brings great comfort to a Christian when seeking assurance of salvation, to know that he or she has repented.

Lastly, Jesus said, 'Make peace with your adversary when you go to war.' In this case he was saying that we must make peace with God whilst on earth, so that He becomes our Friend so that we go to heaven. This means that we must all repent of our sins and obey Jesus.

He also said that, 'Whoever hates his life will lose it, and whoever loses his life for My sake and the gospel will save it.' Hate here means to love less. But the message is clear: Jesus said, 'If someone doesn't give up everything he has, he cannot be My disciple.'

# Chapter Fourteen

## My Baptism

On May nineteenth 1991, with much support and encouragement from my new friends in the Church of Christ (LCC), I was baptised by Patrick Bernard.

I had told my parents I was going to get baptised in Acton in London, and at the Baptistery in Douglas Arthur's garden they brought my godmother and my cousin. My mother was crying, but not with happiness.

Afterwards, I got in my car and drove back to my new friends' shared house in London. There was no one in, so I sat on the wall and said to God, 'Well, I'm not in heaven yet. What shall I do?'

I flicked open the Bible and my eyes lighted on the words *Making Your Calling and Election Sure*, the title in my Bible for 2 Peter 1:10-11. The reading says, '*Make every effort to confirm your calling and election. For if you do these things, you will never stumble, and you will receive a rich welcome into the eternal kingdom of our Lord and Saviour Jesus Christ.*

I then read verses 5-9: *Make every effort to add to your faith goodness; and to goodness, knowledge; and to knowledge, self-control; and to self-control, perseverance; and to perseverance, godliness; and to godliness, brotherly kindness; and to brotherly kindness, love. For if you possess these qualities in increasing measure, they will keep you from being ineffective and unproductive in your knowledge of our Lord Jesus Christ. But whoever does not have them is nearsighted and blind, forgetting that they have been cleansed from their past sins.*

This is the only place in the Bible that says this. It commands us to add these seven qualities to our faith, and then we will receive a rich welcome into heaven.

Through the LCC I learnt about the Great Commission (Matthew 28:18-20) where Jesus commands believers to *'Go and make disciples of all nations, baptising them in the name of the Father and of the Son and of the Holy Spirit, and teaching them to obey everything I have commanded you.'*

This answered my question of what to do with my life, and I decided to answer God's call.

The night after I was baptised I had a dream: I was back with Jesus and His apostles around a camp fire. We all stood in a circle holding a piece of cotton with a thimble on it. It was the children's game of Hunt the Thimble. We all started leaning back on the cotton, and if it 'would' break I 'would' go to hell. Just at the point when it was about to break, Jesus cried out: 'Eloi Eloi lama sabbachtani,' (Aramaic for *My God, My God, why have You forsaken Me?*), which is what He cried on the Cross when He accomplished our salvation. The thread did not break and I woke up knowing I was saved.

Around this time, Patrick invited me in to watch Wimbledon on the TV at Law School. I was reluctant but went in. It was a Ladies' game and I noticed a new dynamic. I felt the temptation of lust to look at the players. I resisted, but the point I make is that I had never felt this to be wrong before. When you are not a Christian, sin is 'normal', but when you are born again, you can see the kingdom of God, and have the Holy Ghost, so sin and temptation are 'unnatural'.

Another dream I had was about five years after salvation. In it I nearly died. I don't mean I dreamt of dying, but that I nearly died in my sleep. I turned to the left and all was black and white, so I turned to the right and started going up a tunnel to heaven and the Great White Light: God. God said to me: 'Do you want to come now, or come later?

This vision is identical to a painting I saw later, for an altarpiece by Hieronymus Bosch that is in the Palazzo Ducale, Venice. The painting has exactly the same colour, dimensions and angle of the tunnel that I saw in my dream.

When God speaks to you, you don't think one thing and say another. What is in your heart is your answer. My answer was, 'I want to work for You. I'll come later.' My mother then came between me and God, and God said, 'Your work is to bring her to Me.'

A third dream I had was in Bristol, when God spoke to me in the way He spoke to Solomon, and asked, 'What do you want?' Asleep, I searched through the Scriptures in my heart looking for what was the best. I remembered where Paul said, 'The only thing that counts is faith expressing itself in love.' (Galatians 5:6.) So I asked that I might do that. God then revealed that I would do that by 'walking by the Holy Spirit.' (Galatians 5:16).

I now know that I was mentally ill at the time, and did not understand why my mind was not working properly. When I was in London living with my friends from the Church of Christ, I caught the Tube to work, cleaning office furniture to pay my way. What a job for a Cambridge graduate! I took the Tube the wrong way a few times, and was greatly distressed by this, but had no idea know what was going on.

Just after I was baptised, when I used to pray together with my new friends, I would get unwelcome thoughts firing at my head, coming from as if they were outside me. I did not know then that this was schizophrenia. I used to shake my head to try and get rid of these 'voices'.

Anyway, I was born again, and the life when I first experienced the kingdom of God was at times frightening. I could see spiritual goings-on, and was very conscious not to sin, even in thought. In fact, I did not knowingly sin for a whole year.

A word of counsel to new Christians. When you first get saved you will find a whole new dynamic going on. The experience of being tempted can be very alarming, but this can be common to all Christians. You are not going through anything unusual, so do not worry. In particular, fellowship meetings with your new Christian brothers and sisters can be quite a challenge, as well as being a wonderful help. Please get involved with a church that teaches the Bible, as soon as you can.

I was baptised and assured of my place in heaven, and my Christian walk began. Three things came into operation: 1. The reading of the Bible, 2. Going to church, and studying the Bible, and 3. I started praying.

The people in the London Church of Christ offered to study the Bible with me. We went through seven topics: Word of God, disciple, sin, repentance, church, worry, and baptism. The 'worry' one was one specially tailored for me.

In 'Word of God' they showed me 'All Scripture is God-breathed and is useful for teaching, rebuking, *correcting and training in righteousness'* (2 Timothy 3:16), and *'No prophecy of Scripture came about by the prophet's own interpretation of things* (2 Peter 1:20). Therefore I saw that the Bible was written by God.

In 'Disciple', I saw the Scripture *'Come, follow Me,' Jesus said, 'and I will send you out to fish for people'* (Matthew 4:19), and the last words of Jesus, *'Therefore go and make disciples of all nations, baptising them in the name of the Father and of the Son and of the Holy Spirit'* (Matthew 28:19. I therefore resolved to preach for life.

With 'Sin', it says that the people confessed before John's baptism. We read in Galatians 5 a list of sins, and I duly confessed: mainly sexual sins.

Then followed 'Repentance' where we saw that worldly sorrow – just being sorry because you've been caught – leads to hell; whereas godly sorrow, sorry because it's wrong, leads to repentance unto salvation.

'Church' we saw is the people – Christians. Not a building.

And lastly, 'Baptism'. We learnt in Romans 6:4 that, *We were therefore buried with him through baptism into death in order that, just as Christ was raised from the dead through the glory of the Father, we too may live a new life.*

Belief in the deity of Christ and repentance are needed to make a baptism effective.

After my baptism I found myself sharing my faith completely naturally, by the Holy Spirit and unforced. This was not because anyone had told me to.

Before my baptism, I had to change a relationship I was in with my girlfriend, although it wasn't physical. So

I finished that relationship and was free. The group had shown me, *'Do not be yoked together with unbelievers. For what do righteousness and wickedness have in common? Or what fellowship can light have with darkness?* (2 Corinthians 6:14).

After getting saved, I witnessed to my old friends but they weren't really interested. I fellowshipped with the Church of Christ and evangelised to everyone.

On the Tube, going in to work on trains absolutely packed with other commuters, I preached from Ecclesiastes chapter 1: 'Everything is meaningless.' I thought that was appropriate.

I asked thousands of City workers if they wanted to come to a Bible discussion with us. A few came. It was during one of them that I decided that I preferred the life of studying the Bible with people, to being a solicitor.

I evangelised at work, and during lunch breaks and afterwards too. Tube preaching is good and I have since done Speakers Corner at Marble Arch, with Bridget. That was good. We witnessed to Muslims who gave me the sign of respect. In fact, I get along very well with them today. They are not atheists, and back in Bristol we always have fruitful theological discussions. About eight have come to salvation in Christ.

While staying with my friends from the Church of Christ when I was a trainee solicitor, the leaders showed me great favour, because I believe that hypocritically they prefer rich people, and they saw me as potentially rich. When I lost my job, things changed.

Mother told me later that she phoned them every day for six months to try and get me out, as she thought they were a cult. They were the most zealous church I have known in twenty-four years, and in one meeting of 1,200 I was mentioned as a disciple who had 'radically repented'. That was the one and only meeting that my parents attended.

I evangelised every house in my home village in Somerset – a thing I have done twice. We used to hold our Bible discussions in various McDonalds in London, and would do one study each time, taking people along the progression that I was taken on.

I have used that system since then, and people have been baptised. Now I give out tracts with the gospel message on. I think this is very effective because people can take it home and read it at their leisure.

The LCC were very pure; I did not spot any sin amongst the twelve hundred members in the whole nine months I was with them. All the men shared houses together, as did the ladies. Every Saturday, we would go out on 'dates'. These were social occasions where a brother would invite a sister on the preceding Sunday meeting, making groups of always at least four. Generally one wouldn't date the same girl twice. We would go typically to a park for lunch or a restaurant for supper. Maybe one glass of wine would be drunk, and sisters had to be back in their houses by midnight.

This degree of supervision, although some may think it to be oppressive, I found worked really well. Couples did get married in the church, and there were excellent relationships in the congregation where the majority of the members were under thirty-five.

At Bible studies, when we prayed, everyone would be on their knees.

Many Christians may have heard of the

Shepherding/pyramid discipling movement. Derek Prince was sucked into this, and it is essentially based on the pyramid selling idea whereby, in the church, the leader disciples several individuals who then disciple more beneath them, etcetera etcetera. I feel that this system is well intentioned, in that the leaders of these particular churches are trying to help the members and keep them out of danger.

I was not actually touched by my disciplers, because I was already doing it all anyway. I have read that some people have complained about the discipling movement in general, and it is clearly open to abuse, given that the discipler has a strong position of influence over his disciples. I personally did not see any such abuse in the LCC.

However, what I seriously do have against the London Church of Christ is their doctrinal error. They told us that if we left the group we would go to hell. We were greatly worried for friends of ours who did leave, and I was terrified for myself also whilst in it, lest I would leave. Note: by the time I did leave (I made my decision in my first mental hospital), all that fear and error had gone.

Incidentally, on a psychological level, consider: what is membership of a group? Going to all the meetings? Adhering to all their doctrines? Being friends with all the members? Etcetera. You can see that there is no easy definition of membership of a group, therefore, and so it can bring fear. The true basis of assurance of salvation is being born again, a Christian, *not membership of any particular church*.

I have discovered that some other churches also hold

this doctrine. I gather this is a form of mind control, and it is highly dangerous. J Lifton formulated the criteria for mind control, and one basis was what he called 'totalitarian society' by which he meant when a group defines itself as having all the answers. And where this is false, clearly there will be great psychological harm to an individual.

This explains why I struggled so much to find my own assurance of salvation during my mental illness. Indeed, when I was admitted to hospital, the doctors told my mother, 'We have seen nothing like it.'

My personality changed: I sadly got rid of all my trendy Thai clothes, and even my handwriting changed (and it still hasn't recovered twenty-four years later). I threw away all my paintings, all my art books, and to my and my mother's distress threw away all my old photos and memorabilia from my years off and Cambridge, including my boxing clothes and tankard.

This rightly distressed all my family that the LCC adversely influenced me to do this, and it is something that I now very much regret.

I have to acknowledge that the LCC helped me considerably in my new Christian life, but since leaving them I have come to see that some of their teaching, their membership requirements and methodology may resemble that of a cult. If you are a member of the LCC, or are considering membership, I urge you to do some research on the internet. You can also contact the Cult Information Centre (http://cultinformation.org.uk/); or write to BCM CULTS, London, WC1N 3XX, UK; or telephone 0845 4500 868 before committing yourself.

# Chapter Fifteen

## The Work of God

The sexual abuse in Hawaii changed the course of my life. I never wanted to be a solicitor, but instead I love street evangelism. Life is important and I wanted, and still do, to work at getting people into heaven. The Bible says that in all things, God works for the good of us who are saved. (Romans 8:28.)

In one exam I fought a battle. I felt led to go out and pray, but on the other hand I remembered my mother's words to be a solicitor. In the end, I opted to stay in the exam. But something happened in my spirit and I thought, *Oh no, have I fallen away?* – which means being condemned to hell. I asked Patrick about this and he said, 'If you *have* fallen away, your old friends will surround you.'

I got home and immediately a Cambridge friend came to see me at Law School, which he hadn't done before, and the guy I met in Thailand phoned me from France. I was *terrified* that I had fallen away. It took me many years to get over this.

I was very afraid, just baptised, and starting to learn the Christian life. One trouble for me has been separating what is due to my mental illness, and what is part of the normal Christian experience. I have heard of someone thinking he was fighting the devil in hell while in bed. I want my readers to understand the terrible suffering the mentally ill can experience, and be sympathetic – not judge or condemn us.

*God* rescued me from extreme mental illness, and

baptised me. I was on a journey, but didn't know it. The great thing is that there is an answer. So if you too are struggling with life, I am telling you that Jesus is there, and He is the answer.

I have travelled the same journey that Christians for two thousand years have been witnessing to – that Jesus is God, and will forgive your sins and take care of you.

*If we claim to be without sin, we deceive ourselves and the truth is not in us. If we confess our sins, he is faithful and just and will forgive us our sins and purify us from all unrighteousness. If we claim we have not sinned, we make him out to be a liar and his word is not in us* (1 John 1:8-10).

Today, we witness to those people who are still travelling. They may be afraid, uncertain and unhappy, but becoming a Christian is the answer, both in this life and forever. Hallelujah. I have been through the pain, and want to save you from it. Just ask Jesus for a place in heaven, join a church, read the Bible and pray. That is why the message of the Bible is called *Good News*, and why Christians in parts of the world are willing to die to tell people about it.

Jesus commands all to spread the gospel. However, for you it may not be full-time speaking like me, but your priority must be to share your faith. St Paul made tents for a living, but his heart was to save people. My message to you is that you must repent to enter heaven. That means to give up sin and follow Jesus. He commands that we spread the gospel as a lifestyle. If you are sitting in an office wondering what to do, there is a really exciting life available for you.

While at The Downs School, the gospel was

preached daily at Morning Assembly, and at one particular one I recall knowing that I already had faith by then (aged about eleven). I prayed for a short while, but had no real awakening until I was twenty-four. I had two prior leadings of God to Him. First, at BGS aged fourteen, I thought of going to the Christian Union, but thought they were too wet. I was in the rugby team and thought that was better.

Secondly, at Cambridge, Erik and Emma invited me to Christians in Sport. There, the preacher said we should not look at women. That is exactly what I was doing (albeit only at their eyes) so I didn't respond. Looking back, I can see what sin and pain I could have avoided if I had turned to God at an earlier age.

By then, after a life of sin, I was on my knees in the metaphorical sense. I was mentally ill. I failed my mock solicitor's exams dismally, but God (hallelujah) rescued me. He provided Himself. He is the answer. He provided a new life in Christ – through Jesus' death for me on the cross – which I accepted and grabbed one hundred percent

The Bible says that God grants repentance, and mine had begun. I stopped being a fornicator as I realized there was no love in it. I also decided to 'go the whole hog' and stopped masturbating.

When you give up sin, of course, you have to put something in its place. For the first time, I thought about what to do with my life. As I was at Law School I thought of becoming an Amnesty International lawyer, but they required two years post-qualification experience which was five years away for me.

Then I thought of being a solicitor with a 'social law

firm' doing immigration, housing etc for the poor, but they also required that I apply two years in advance. I then thought of becoming a (homeopathic) doctor, but that required £8,500.

I had a contract with a top City firm but was not interested in just making loads of money.

I got my life in order and started to pray at night. Within three days God started to work and I had immediate answers to prayer.

God leads us by the Holy Spirit to share our faith with everyone. So *this* is God's will for Christians. First get your place in heaven, and then get others in.

While I was getting closer to God and learning from teaching in the church, I read a book on comparative religion which had some wisdom that helped me. God used it on my path.

Incidentally, when I got saved and read in the Bible that to get healed one must go to the elders and get anointed with oil and be prayed for, I wrote to my homeopath and told her what I now believed. I cancelled my treatment with her and threw away all my homeopathic pills.

Repentance – a gift from Almighty God – must encompass your whole life, not merely a few sins. God was producing personal changes in my life; I started taking a lot of care in my life with cooking and other daily tasks. And when I had 'got my life right' I sought to share it. 'Take care, and share'. That was when I tried to move into a shared house, and Patrick came along.

# Chapter Sixteen

## Life in London

I was accepted by the top six English solicitors' firms and chose Freshfields. When I got there after Law School in 1991 I was already saved, but unknowingly suffering from schizophrenia. I couldn't even work a photocopier without attacks to my head in the form of voices. I managed to do the work though – just – and I think they were pleased.

While at Freshfields, some friends asked me to go to a bar in Fleet Street with them. They were using insulting, filthy language about the women who would be there. So I didn't go. (I think they're all married now.)

Another guy at Guildford, a Jew, when I was having a stressful mental health time, invited me up to his room and offered me a pornographic video. I turned on my heel and left without it. This confirmed me more to follow Christ, not the world.

Law School results come out six weeks into our Articles contract, and mine was a fail. I was called up to the senior partner's room that morning and the recruitment partner was there with him. They asked me, 'Is this job the most important thing in your life?'

I said no.

They said, 'It is for all of us here. Clear your desk by this afternoon.' And then as I was leaving they said, 'We're Christians too, you know.'

They also said, 'Come back when you've passed Law School,' but that's something I never did. They gave me £2,000 as I left.

I tried to pass Law School again. I went to a Crammers, but my mind just would not work. In 1994 I re-sat what was then the Legal Practice Course at UWE, and narrowly failed, passing fifteen out of sixteen exams. It seemed that I was just destined not to be a solicitor. It wasn't until four years later that I was told by Jesus to street evangelise full-time.

After Freshfields, I started looking for jobs in central London. I found one at Debenhams and went for the interview. Halfway through, the woman asked me if I enjoyed sales assistant work, because I had done it before. I remember thinking, *If I say yes it will be a lie, but if I say no I won't get the job.* I told the truth and said no ... and she offered me the job!

I continued to preach the gospel, and was fired from Debenhams for witnessing. I recall I couldn't even work the till without interruption from schizophrenic voices. Then followed vain attempts at employment, and eventual signing-on.

When I lost my job, my flat mate said he would pay my way, but I think the church leaders got to hear of this and didn't like it. My discipler suddenly gave me an Old Testament Scripture out of the blue, saying 'A wise son pleases his mother' and it was said in an unfriendly way.

The leaders probably discovered I was on benefit, and one day said, 'Go home and learn responsibility.' I was out.

I returned to Bristol as part of a Church of Christ church plant there, and my mother got me into a day-care mental hospital. They then put me in a full mental home and I was sectioned. I told my London church friends of this just before I was driven off in an ambulance, and once there, I phoned one of them in London. He just said, 'Don't you trust God?' and put the phone down.

Not once did they phone, write to or visit me, and I never heard from them again.

When I was first put in the mental day-care hospital, at one of the sessions on feelings, after many personal feelings had been mentioned, I piped up and said, 'This all seems to prove the truth of Jeremiah in the Bible who said, 'The heart is deceitful above all things, and beyond cure. Who can know it?''

At that, the boss, a Catholic nun, marched me down to her office and asked me, 'How do you feel?' I felt nothing, which I later gathered is a recognized medical symptom. So I, rather wittily I thought, replied, 'I feel with my fingertips. How do you feel?'

She was not amused and said, 'Would you like to go into the mental hospital?'

They threw me into a mental hospital and I was cut off from all fellowship, and my mind was filled with very odd medication.

In Bristol I had a delusion that I was in the bottomless pit (Revelation 20:1). Another day I had a delusion that I was fighting to get into heaven but couldn't, because the door was shut. I persevered with God however, and eventually the Holy Spirit dwelling in me got me under the door. God showed me by this that it is only by His grace and the Holy Spirit living in us, and not by our own works, that we enter heaven.

God confirmed His move in my life by many miracles. They were minor, but telling. One amazing miracle I had, about two years after my baptism, was when I was doing a thousand piece jig-saw puzzle. I was averaging one piece every twenty-five minutes because the picture was so complicated. And then I thought of the Scripture, 'Keep your eyes fixed on Jesus'. I did this and suddenly put five pieces in a row in about as many seconds.

I have peace about work now and get joy every time I street evangelise. I want to do it, and it fulfils everything I ever wanted in a job. I work with people outside, and do the best thing in the world: spreading the gospel and trying to get people into heaven. Hallelujah.

Bridget and I are available to speak in churches or anywhere. We work together, and most of our results have come that way. She has helped me immensely.

A word to those seeking a career: Jesus said keep seeking and you will find (Matthew 7:7). At age sixteen at BGS I did a career aptitude test. With my background I put down jobs like accountant, but I also liked being outside in the sun, so I put bricklayer etc. Not surprisingly it was inconclusive, as bricklaying and accountancy do not mix.

For the next seventeen years I sought what to do with my life. With my Cambridge degree, I looked at everything – politician, civil servant, teacher etc. Then in 2000 Jesus gave me street evangelism, so don't give up, you can find your niche.

A word also about drugs: I am totally against them. They often cause mental illness. They mess you up, cause people to lose their life focus, and can make you vulnerable to other risks. I have had none for over twenty years. They are also against the law.

After losing my Debenhams job I was out looking for

jobs on the streets; I worked for a short time with a LCC solicitor and we tried to get a client off Death Row in America. Then I attempted to tutor a Jewish man doing his first year of Law School. I visited him a couple of times at his house in Hampstead, but resigned because I felt I wasn't sufficiently qualified to take him all the way.

Bridget and I returned to Guildford on a mission ten years after I left. We parked in the College and they locked us in. I went to the nearest telephone and made calls in vain because no one could help. I was distressed, but by the time I retuned to the College car park, I found Bridget had 'opened' the padlock with an iron bar she kept in the car, and I was mighty relieved.

Evangelising with Bridget on Whiteladies Road in Bristol

# Chapter Seventeen

## My Post-Baptism Walk

My main difficulty post-baptism was keeping on my 'Helmet of Salvation' (Ephesians 6), i.e. maintaining my assurance of salvation.

I did not live that morally for a long time. My immediate post-baptism was okay but, when I was later sectioned, things definitely went downhill.

Being incarcerated and therefore prevented from street evangelism, I fell into masturbation (initially, 'to see if everything still worked', was the deception the enemy used). Then I was tempted and deceived into sexual relationships. While a patient, I was seduced by a nurse. She had invited me back to her flat while I was on leave. Up till then I had stayed moral as a Christian. A few other girlfriends then followed. I am now out of all these, but I cost myself some Christian maturity in not walking by the Holy Spirit but by the flesh.

There is only *one* way to stop: *STOP!*

Prayer helps, and confession to God and a fellow believer is mandatory. God grants repentance. Go on your knees with your face to the floor and beg God for His forgiveness. Stay there until you get repentance.

My sinful life continued, despite my efforts to resist, until I met Bridget. She discerned that the people around me were what we diagnosed as 'the gutter press'. She helped me get rid of them, and my life truly blossomed afterwards – thousands saved, radio interviews, twenty-five baptisms, and I don't look ill as I used to. I have now abstained from sex for over twelve years, and have got my life back on track.

God disciplines after sin. This is not pleasant, as the Bible says (Hebrews 12), and must be borne: 'Strengthen the weak knees'.

Oh what wonders could be ours if we all obeyed God and kept our eyes on Jesus all the time.

As a Christian, I now lead a moral life, although this has been difficult to achieve after falling badly after my baptism. I have to say that the change only comes from *you* and *God*. No one can do it for you. The desire for change has to come from within. This is true with all repentance. Friends can help, but it is ultimately between you and God.

Before I was saved, I admit I actively sought relationships, but afterwards, although I fell into them, I was trying not to. In my second year off I had a number of short-term relationships. This is damaging as it is outside God's will and as I said earlier, once a physical relationship is started, it should not end 'till death do part.' i.e. marriage.

When Bridget met me, my feet were stuck in mud. This was from wrong relationships with the 'gutter press'. As Yeshua said: 'where there is a dead body, the vultures gather'. Throughout this time I evangelised to everyone, went regularly to church, prayed continually and studied the bible full-time. That is why I think I got through the trouble- its like an arrow going in the right direction; despite the sin, the arrow (me) kept going because I was doing the right basics.

Because I was stuck in mud (sin), I needed Bridget to help me get out. She was given many words by God of how these gutter press were damaging me. Every time she suggested a step to get out, I took it.

I operated an open house and always had a pot on the stove. The trouble was these people took advantage and would stay from morning till past midnight, eating and drinking all the time. When I would go for an afternoon nap, they wouldn't even leave and would still be there when I woke up.

Also, people took advantage of my mental illness- I was unable to say no or stick up for myself. Once I had to walk out of my own flat because a man was verbally abusing me.

These immoral Christians were extremely hard to get rid of. We had to write letters, get a gate put at the bottom of my garden, and tell them many times to leave me alone.

There are a number of points here: one, keep doing the Christian basics at all times. Two, if you're in bad sin you may need the active help of another Christian to get you free. Three, be prepared, as a good Christian, to become actively involved if you want to rescue and help a Christian in need.

I finally did put a stop to them all coming round when I felt that my need exceeded theirs.

My initial sexual repentance came without hearing any Christian teaching. It must have been the Holy Spirit working with me direct: which is great.

I have never really been into porn (a few times). Amongst other problems, it is impersonal. Someone can't have a relationship with a photograph. They are robbing themselves. So don't.

I was appointed as an elder when I ran a house-church in my Bristol flat, called The Way. We had twelve members and met twice a week for one and a half years. The average attendance was four or five, which is just right for a flat sitting room. I now hold meetings once a week which we call *God Knows Best*. We start at 7:30 pm and often continue until after midnight, sometimes till dawn. About four come on average, and we fellowship, pray and have Communion. All are welcome.

I have also been 'sent-out' with hands being laid on me by Bridget, a prophetess – the most godly Christian I know. I felt God's touch and things were different immediately. I seemed to have a power over sin. My credentials are that I have studied the Bible every day for twenty-four years since my baptism, plus reading related literature, and I now believe I have a sound understanding of Christian doctrine, but I feel I still have more to learn about living it.

I have received the baptism in the Holy Ghost. One Lord's Day at Pip 'n' Jay church in Bristol the vicar, Malcolm Widdecombe, described what this baptism was like. Two weeks later I was lying on my bed in the afternoon and exactly what he described happened to me. I wasn't expecting, seeking or even thinking about it. All of a sudden a spiritual fountain of silvery, sparkling 'water' came up out of my heart and cascaded over my head. It was beautiful, and I was filled with ecstasy.

I have the gift of prophecy, from the Holy Spirit, and have been filled with the Holy Spirit since my baptism.

When in the year 2000 I was street evangelising part-time, I was still seeking a career. Then one day, whilst thinking about street evangelism, I said to Jesus, 'All right, I will do it full-time.' And I got peace from heaven in my heart, and I knew God was saying, 'Yes, that's what I want you to do.'

Secondly, I was lying in bed one night, searching for 'a place for my thoughts' – if you know what I mean. A place of rest. I had been doing this in vain for about two years. Suddenly the word *apostle* came into my mind. I received a beautiful peace and knew Jesus was calling me to be an apostle.

Later, God confirmed this to Bridget and another friend by a flash, similar to lightning, Bridget says, even though there was no storm. This happened just as she said to our friend, 'I think Simon is an apostle.' Bridget and I regularly witness signs and wonders happening around me, which is a biblical mark of apostleship.

Every time I evangelise, I immediately get filled with joy and I do it without being paid. I once heard a rock star say he would do his job even if he wasn't paid for it. Well, I have that too, and *I* don't get paid for it!

It fulfils my earlier desire for a job with people and the outdoors. Also, it's the best job in the world, trying to get people into heaven. Hallelujah.

As I have already said, I have no human boss, and I can choose my own hours and have no restrictions or orders on how to do it – except under God, of course.

Even though I had a rather chequered walk after the first year after baptism and fell sexually and suffered with mental ill health, God never left me.

I co-ran a drop-in for the poor in Bristol with Bridget, called The Shepherd's Tent. I baptised eighteen people in four years, and persevered with evangelism. I have attended church, read the Bible and prayed throughout my Christian walk.

At The Shepherd's Tent, the word of God was shared with *everyone* who came in, around 500 people. Many homeless took leaflets with them to give out on their travels, putting them under car windscreen wipers, and passing them on to other homeless.

*'Be as innocent as doves and as wise as a serpent'.* When Bridget and I began working with the homeless we were as innocent as doves (as Jesus said), but now we are now also learning the wisdom. Consequently, we are now able to witness and minister on the streets, often at night to crowds, and we are helping many mentally ill people. Another scripture that springs to mind is 'take the plank out of your own eye, and then you will see clearly to take the speck out of another's.'

The homeless at the Tent often tried to take advantage of us, but we protected each other. Now, after much experience, we are, by God's grace, able to read people, understand their psychology and not get drawn into traps. We have both learned to say no, which is absolutely crucial if you are going to do Christian ministry, and keep our boundaries.

Note: it is not for no reason that Jesus sent the 12 and 72 out in pairs: there is great protection.

Bridget and I could teach much on this, and indeed we are just starting seminars, called Living Flame, to try and pass on what we have learned.

Around 150,000 leaflets have been given out by Bridget and me. At least 2,000 people have called on the Lord for salvation to my knowledge; and I believe a lot more have found Jesus in the quiet of their own homes.

About ten years ago I got rid of my TV. As well as saving Â£160 p.a., I also gained 2 hours per day. I gave it up mainly because the shows were so banal and I also couldn't take all the continual bad news. With the time saved, I immediately turned my overgrown garden into organic fruit and vegetables. This is definitely something I recommend.

After the mental hospitals I attended Anglican churches: first the local one I grew up next to, in our Somerset village, and then three in Bristol, when I moved there. That was for a total of twelve years. I know the New Testament and am familiar with the Old.

I recommend following Acts 3:1; this is the hour of prayer between 3-4 pm. I do, and have for over 10 years. For several, I did so on my knees and prayed for souls to be saved (which is my habitual prayer). Then God led Bridget and me to our youth outreach and thousands are being saved. It was then that we received an anointing for street- evangelism. Whole groups will pray for salvation and repent together. On College Green we were surrounded by crowds of up to 30 all firing questions at us, and by the grace of God we answered them all. Two things I found are required: 1. Know the bible, and 2. Have the courage to speak it.

People would pray for salvation and then run and get their friends and either lead them in the prayer or bring them to us. They would invite us to stay in their heavenly mansion and say we were their spiritual 'parents'- this without us saying that- they seemed to know the scriptures already. They would say we were the grand-parents of their converts. This is revival. Tongues and interpretation fell, one guy jumped in the pool to be baptised and tens of thousands of pieces of Christian literature were given out. Glory to GOD.

After 3 years, from drugs, drunkenness and witchcraft, every single one of them wanted Jesus. Trainee Anglican vicars came down and joined in. God told me that the kingdom of God had been established there and we have never been back.

The anointing of God always remains and we had the same results at skate-board parks and do at McDonalds, Burger King etc. People are wide open for the gospel, especially youth, who are still seeking. Also lately, we find revellers are, of all ages. They all want to know and often pray for salvation.

So go out and spread Jesus. I pray you find the same results. You will find evidence of this revival in our earliest You Tube videos (under Simonbridget).

\* \* \*

Bridget and I have recently been asked to join the Board of a new Church called Bread, being started by Alwyn Pereira, a good friend, who is also a Church of England curate. We are excited by this.

SIMON FARRIS

LOG ON NOW: www.newlife.co.uk

# Goths are targeted by couple

TWO preachers claim to have seen more than 400 Goths become Christians in Bristol.

Simon Farris and Bridget White distribute Gospel tracts most weeks in the city, as they reach out to help the normally criticised Goth community.

Simon, a law graduate from Cambridge University, says he and close friend Bridget have a burning desire to fulfil the work of God.

The 40-year-old told New Life: "The Bible says that whoever calls upon the name of the Lord shall be saved. We are seeing real things happen. People are giving their lives to Christ. I had a Jew pray the prayer recently and a Muslim a few weeks ago. Things are really happening.

"Jesus commissioned me to street evangelism about eight years ago, and ever since I was baptised when I was 24, I have followed the Great Commission.

"We teach the Goths about morality and tell them to get off drink and drugs and to dress modestly. They're in the early stages of Christianity, and are asking a lot of questions. Some have even said they want to be baptised."

One convert, 14-year-old Paul Kingston, told New Life: "I've made a fresh commitment to Christianity. I'm now looking at when I can be baptised."

*New Life* newspaper 2008

# STUDENT REVOLUTION

## 1,700 young people give lives to Christ on Bristol's streets

A CAMBRIDGE graduate gave up his career to share the good news about Jesus with the youth of Bristol – and now 1,700 people have been rescued from alcohol abuse, drugs and even Satanism.

Simon Farris and his co-worker, Bridget White, have been engaging with young people in and around Bristol for five years, and over that time have seen more than 1,700 students and other young people turn to Christ.

Although Simon and Bridget have met their fair share of scepticism and mockery, they have also found a hunger for spiritual truth. Simon says: "We have met a lot of Goths and other teenagers on drink and drugs, involved in promiscuity. But after we have talked to those who are willing to listen, about 80 per cent ask Jesus to save them and change their lives.

"Often whole groups would believe together; we've had a wide variety of people getting saved, including Satanists, Muslims, Jews and homosexuals."

Simon and Bridget started their Christian outreach while running a drop-in for the homeless. During that time, 16 of the homeless people became Christians and were baptised. They then began to work full time on the streets, talking to young people wherever they found them.

### Problem

We are used to the media telling us that most young people aren't interested in Christianity and atheism is on the rise, but Simon is finding this simply isn't true. The real problem is that many British youth simply haven't heard the Christian message explained to them properly before, and when they do understand many are open. Simon explains: "We believe that the youth in the Western world are wide open for the Christian message now. If you mention the reality of heaven to them, and that the way to get there is through Jesus, they immediately become interested and keen to talk.

"We've often been surrounded by up to 30 teenagers at a time, all firing questions, all wanting to know the truth. People are getting saved all the time."

Simon is a Cambridge University law graduate who has sacrificed a lucrative career to share something much more valuable with people – the transforming power of Jesus. Simon recalls: "I decided 20 years ago to devote myself to Jesus' command to go out into the world and lead people to him, rather than pursue my solicitor's career that I had set up in the City.

### Trusting

"I've believed in Jesus since childhood – I don't know when I first started trusting him. But looking back, I can remember being called to follow him on three occasions. The third was when I was at law school, training to be a solicitor, aged 23, in 1991. God's Holy Spirit worked upon my heart, showed me my need to stop sinning against God, and drew me towards a life of serving Christ.

"But there was one sin I still felt guilty about, even though I knew Jesus was offering forgiveness. I was paranoid about something I had done in Hawaii during a

**TAKING THE GOSPEL TO THE STREETS:**
Simon Farris (left) talks about faith with young people in Bristol

year off from university. The guilt would only go away after downing a couple of pints. But I knew I could not carry on living like that, so I decided to give up all drugs – not just alcohol, cigarettes and marijuana (which I took a lot of in Thailand), but even the mild ones like tea and coffee. The next morning I woke up symptom-free, and the guilt has never returned.

"Next I decided to stop sleeping with my girlfriend, as the Bible teaches that sex is only for marriage.

### Meaningful

"So, not being happy with just lining my own pockets as a solicitor, I looked for something more meaningful to do. I thought about being an Amnesty International lawyer, but they required two years' experience. So I tried a 'social' law firm doing housing, immigration, etc., but they required I apply in two years' time, so I looked at being a doctor.

"But then I started praying for guidance, and I began to get direct answers from God. Having cleaned up my life, God really started to work on me! I read in the Bible that Jesus wants Christians to tell people about him, and I knew that was what I wanted to do with my life.

"It's then that I started street-evangelising [telling people on the streets about Jesus], at first part time, and then full time."

As a result, Simon and Bridget have started a church in Bristol, and feel God is leading them to start another in London.

Good *News* newspaper 2012

97

# Chapter Eighteen

## My Experience of Mental Illness

I was sectioned twice, for seven months and later for six months. I contend that there were no legal grounds for this as I was on prescribed medication, compliant at all times, both before, during, and after my detention.

I was given ECT several times, always against my will. This involves sending 1,200 volts through the brain, and it induces an epileptic fit.

I was also given drugs causing a sort of paralysis when I was first admitted, making my body go stiff, and making my muscles force my head to the right so I could hardly move it. This was done without warning me in advance of the side effects. A friend was given medication that made him go blue, and he stopped breathing.

Whilst locked up, I was subject to a nurse who tried to destroy my faith. For three days I was unable to get away, while he tried to work on my mind.

The sections, for schizophrenia, actually caused me to get depression, as I was prevented from working as a solicitor or anything else. I had depression then for four years, which is absolutely terrible and I thank God that one day it just lifted.

I had met the Bristol TV weatherman on the street, and he said, 'Keep your eyes on the end of the tunnel.' My depression was in the heart, not the head. My medication did not help at all.

The legal grounds for a section are:

a)   Someone is mentally ill, and

b) It is for their benefit, or to avoid harm to another.

In a tribunal I was declared not to be a danger to others, and as for 'harm to myself', case law says the least requirement is that someone refuses to take prescribed medication. As I said, before I was sectioned I had already been taking medication for a month, and never did I refuse it while in hospital.

I think the mental health authorities should go a lot further in getting patients' agreement before they medicate. Also, I am sure that much healing can be achieved through counselling. No doctor got to the bottom of why I was ill. To do that, it took Bridget who prayed for me, and I am now liberated.

After my release, I wrote to Simon Brittain, the head psychiatrist at Barrow Gurney mental hospital suggesting that fifty percent of healing could be achieved by 'talking therapy'. He invited me to come and talk to the staff about this idea, saying he was impressed by the non-condemnation in my letter. I heard later that my recommendation had been implemented.

A female friend was strip searched when she was in hospital, by men and women. I consider this a gross violation of her human rights and dignity, which I would like to prosecute in the courts.

They also injected me, and others, in the backside. This, I believe, is degrading treatment under Article 3 of the Human Rights Act. At the time, my psychiatrist told me that it is just as effective in the upper arm, so why was it done this way?

Almost every patient I have met complains about their treatment by the mental health services. Doesn't that tell you something? Of course, medication can be effective in the right circumstances. However, it must not be administered in a violent way. Jesus healed, but He committed no violence. Yes, God has made healing substances, and they can work for many people.

In the Gospels, insane people did have the presence of mind to ask Jesus for healing. God can get through to someone, whatever state they are in.

It is worth noting that mentally ill people are often in touch with Jesus. Psychiatrists wrongly interpret this by saying that religious people are mad. They did with me. I was told, 'We believe you are mentally ill – because you talk about Jesus.' I would say, 'On the contrary. The Bible says, 'God is close to the broken-hearted and to those who especially need His help.''

My present medication has got rid of some of my schizophrenic symptoms, and as such I willingly take it. However, it is not a perfect solution. It would be far better to be totally healed. For this to happen, perhaps further counselling would be useful. I tried Cognitive Behavioural Treatment, but found it no help at all.

Mental health workers need to respect all rights of the individual. From my own experience I have to say that you don't help someone unless you do – you just make things worse. The whole person must be cared for: mind, body and spirit.

In particular, I have noted that those in the psychiatric profession need to acknowledge the validity of the Christian faith. For example, a good Christian friend of mine says his psychiatrist told him that he believes St Paul was mentally ill regarding his Damascus Road experience, and he would have sectioned him.

I was ill because, while under the influence of drugs, I was molested in Hawaii by a homosexual predator, but they thought it was due to my membership of the Church of Christ, and never asked me about it. I had schizophrenia, but they gave me depression by locking me up. I was first detained in high security wards, as though I was some sort of criminal. Plastic windows and twenty-four hour surveillance.

All I was doing, when I was taken to hospital the second time, was quietly playing a game of chess with my dad. I was doped out for three days and nights, and all I can remember is being woken up regularly and fed a pink liquid. Why? It is oppression.

One of the worst things about a section is there is no guarantee of release. At least a prisoner knows when he is getting out, but a patient has to rely on the whim of the psychiatrist, which may never come.

I never refused medication, but I didn't like the injections. Humiliating. I protested and five nurses jumped on me, held me down, and injected me.

Does incarceration do more harm or good? I was never violent, and it was agreed at the outset that I was no danger to others. Do people really think that a drug will get to the bottom of why someone is mentally ill? *No!* There is a cause. They say for schizophrenia there is a genetic weakness, plus trauma, plus a trigger.

My trauma was that I was on my own in Hawaii, had just had everything stolen, had no money, no passport and no flight ticket home. And then the trigger was molestation by a homosexual. But they didn't ask.

Just pills? How ridiculous. No talk, no therapy, no counselling.

If you are mentally ill, Bridget and I will talk to you, and pray and give all the help we can, if you want it. We have helped numerous mentally ill people. They all were or became friends. We counsel and listen. People respond to us and get better and recommend us to their friends.

I am in favour of medication. God has made healing substances, and I take Olanzapine, a brilliant anti-schizophrenic medicine which has sorted out the 'positive' symptoms – as they are called – like the delusions, voices (auditory hallucinations) and visual hallucinations which I had before.

A psychiatrist once told me that to achieve mental health, one needs to have balance, rhythms and patterns in life. Many Christian psychiatrists say, *One can only achieve wholeness when sin has gone, and when guilt has been removed by God's forgiveness.* It is guilt that drives many people to them for help.

So-called 'negative symptoms' can include general loss of enjoyment of life, and loss of interest. Also, reduced energy and decreased activity with not much motivation. These symptoms I still have. So please pray for me. Medication can't touch these negative symptoms. However, I *am* interested in God's things: street evangelism which is my work, for example.

Something Bridget and I have noticed in our many dealings with mentally ill people, and also through reading, that sexual abuse is a *very* common cause of mental illness.

Do not think that my experience in two mental hospitals was unique. Abuse of all forms is still taking place. Hidden cameras placed in care homes and institutions by concerned relatives have revealed ongoing and serious physical, sexual, and mental abuse of vulnerable people of all ages, often leading to prosecutions in the courts, and in some cases closure.

One thing I noticed whilst severely ill was that people encroach upon your borders. One has natural boundaries, and when ill you are less able to protect them. When my delusions and hallucinations stopped due to medication, I found I had to regain that territory that I had lost.

Lately, Bridget and I have been supported by the NHS Bristol Community Access Support Service who have linked us in with all the mental health organisations in the city so we can provide them for our clients. That is useful.

# Chapter Nineteen

## Healings of Myself and Others

I have had three healings for myself:

I had back pain for as long as I could remember, and asked three Christians, including Bridget and the owner of The Shepherd's Tent, Sally Jackson, to pray. I felt something correct itself in my spine and have had no pain since, and that was many years ago.

Secondly, I got something in my eye. While we were on the way to the hospital, we were praying. Then I remembered that Job prayed for his friends. So just as I was praying for all people with eye problems, I felt something happen under my eyelid, like it was flipping something out. And the pain was gone. Hallelujah.

For others:

One man claims his tooth was healed. At The Shepherd's Tent, Bridget and I were thinking of advertising meetings WITH HEALINGS POSSIBLE. But I said, 'No, I'm not going to say that, because we've prayed for so many without success.'

However, the very next day we went into The Tent and someone was instantly healed of constipation (he actually drank the anointing oil in faith) and immediately ran to the bathroom and was healed. Praise the Lord.

We felt God was definitely saying, 'Yes, you do have healings attached to your ministry.'

I have kept evangelising, reading the Bible, going to church and praying. It is extremely important for Christians to do this. We created a Bristol Good Church

Guide on the Internet and local radio, and have put on revival meetings for the homeless.

Looking back at life before I was a Christian, why did I sin? The reason was, I think, because the opportunity was there. I drank alcohol because it was available. I took drugs because I was offered them. I think this may be why many people do it. It may be partly due to the lack of ethical and moral teaching these days. We are taught complex sums, and to speak foreign languages, but not the basics like relationships, or seeing right from wrong. I think money management should be taught too. When I became mentally ill, I found I ran up large debts.

In summary, I believe that God was calling me from a young age, but He especially started to work in my second year off. Then I repented at Law School. Note that this was without any Christians around, or even having a Bible. I was repenting by the action of the Holy Spirit on me. Then God got me a Bible, brought me Patrick and the Church of Christ, and I was baptised.

In spite of my subsequent reservations about the London Church of Christ, God works in all things for the good of Christians. For me, the abuse in Hawaii turned my life from being a solicitor, which I didn't want to be, to street evangelism which I love.

I have an anointing for street evangelism from God, and people are getting saved all the time. Bridget and I have revival and we get crowds all taking leaflets and wanting to talk about GOD. The harvest, as Jesus said, is truly 'bountiful'.

# Chapter Twenty

## Why Preach?

*When one of the Pharisees invited Jesus to have dinner with him, he went to the Pharisee's house and reclined at the table. A woman in that town who lived a sinful life learned that Jesus was eating at the Pharisee's house, so she came there with an alabaster jar of perfume. As she stood behind him at his feet weeping, she began to wet his feet with her tears. Then she wiped them with her hair, kissed them and poured perfume on them. When the Pharisee who had invited him saw this, he said to himself, 'If this man were a prophet, he would know who is touching him and what kind of woman she is – that she is a sinner.'*

*Jesus answered him, 'Simon, I have something to tell you.'*

*'Tell me, teacher,' he said.*

*'Two people owed money to a certain moneylender. One owed him five hundred denarii, and the other fifty. Neither of them had the money to pay him back, so he forgave the debts of both. Now which of them will love him more?'*

*Simon replied, 'I suppose the one who had the bigger debt forgiven.'*

*'You have judged correctly,' Jesus said.*

*Then Jesus turned toward the woman and said to Simon, 'Do you see this woman? I came into your house. You did not give me any water for my feet, but she wet my feet with her tears and wiped them with her hair. You did not give me a kiss, but this woman, from the time I entered, has not stopped kissing my feet. You did not put oil on my head, but she has poured perfume on my feet. Therefore, I tell you, her many sins have been forgiven – as her great love has shown. But whoever has been forgiven little loves little'* (Luke 7:36-47).

I can identify with that woman. In her community she would have been brought up to know about God, and like me she had a life without God. Then she met Jesus. He washed her completely clean of all her past. No wonder she loved much. No wonder she was not afraid or ashamed to show her love for Jesus.

Now that I have experienced God's amazing, undeserved forgiveness through the death of Jesus on the cross, how can I do anything except share this with others full time, and tell them that God in His love wants to forgive them too? I have evangelised everyone I have met since my baptism.

So all glory to God.

My car was being driven by Bridget one day, and a man we later saw at church told us that he was witnessing to a Muslim who said, 'I will not believe unless I see it written.' At that moment Bridget drove by, he saw my car, and immediately gave his life to Jesus and was baptised a few weeks later. He was the son of an Imam.

# Questions and a Prayer

Where do you see yourself in life? As someone who is not too bad, someone who is certainly not as bad as many other people you know, someone who has probably done enough good things in life to get a place in heaven? Let me tell you that your good works will not save you.

Or are you ready to come to Jesus now to confess your sins and ask for His forgiveness? Do you want to be *sure* of a place in heaven? Then pray this prayer. Remember, Jesus died on the cross and took *your* punishment.

*'Dear Jesus, I know I am a sinner. I thank You for dying on the cross for me. I've done nothing to earn Your love, but I believe in my heart that You are the Son of God. I believe that God raised You from the dead, and I confess You with my mouth. Please forgive me my sins and wash my heart clean. Come and live in my life, be the Lord of my life, and fill me with Your Holy Spirit. Teach me to walk with You and live for You the rest of my life. Thank You for saving me and for giving me the gift of eternal life in heaven with You. Amen.'*

Or did you pray a prayer like this once, but have now turned your back on God and gone your own way? It's not too late to turn back, confess, and receive a loving welcome from your Heavenly Father, just like the Prodigal Son in the story that Jesus told in Luke 15:11-32. Remember, *if we confess our sins, He is faithful and just and will forgive us our sins and purify us from all unrighteousness* (1 John 1:8-9). God is waiting. Come back now.

# Summary by Bridget White

I first met Simon in 2001, when he came into the Elmgrove Centre for the homeless in Bristol where I worked. Right from the first meeting, I felt that there was something special about him. I later found out he went to Cambridge University, and had been hoping to be a solicitor, but after going abroad on a gap year out and experiencing some difficulties in his life, he started to look for a deeper meaning in his own life. He persevered, and found God. He soon found out God was calling him, in the midst of all the education and travelling.

Just when he was about to enter Law School in Guildford to study for a year, before he started his career as a solicitor in London, Simon began to search even deeper. He got a Bible in a shop after going there for another book. Some time later he went to a church in London and was baptised. Then Simon was commissioned by God to Street Evangelise. This is what Simon was doing when I met him in 2001.

He started a six week prayer meeting with me and about eight others at the Elmgrove Centre, an old Anglican Church on Redland Road in Cotham, Bristol.

I had been told by God to go beside 'The Shepherd's Tent' (Song of Solomon 1:8) and there 'tend the flock of my inheritance' (Micah 7:14). When deciding the name of the drop-in, Simon, not knowing of the word I had received, suggested Shepherd's Hut. Someone else then suggested Shepherd's Tent. So we knew that this was confirmation that our venture was from God. Soon it had lots of homeless men and women coming in for food. We ran it as a church. Simon was very gifted with the homeless and soon was popular. Many got baptised by him in the drop-in. I discovered that things went much better when Simon was there.

At times when I ran it with others it was okay, but not spiritual, so I approached Simon with this, and he became a very committed worker. After the drop-in shut down after four years, God gave us a word to go out on the streets to reach the young teenagers.

It was then we went to College Green where a few hundred of them met every Saturday. We went there every Saturday for three years until another church took over. One boy was baptised by Simon, and many others have gone to local churches. We also travelled around to small villages in and around Bristol, as well as going to Ireland, Wales and the Isle of Wight.

Simon continued his evangelism in a very busy and dangerous part of Bristol where drink and drugs are the norm. Sometimes violence can erupt, but he kept going and handing out tracts showing the way to God.

Then God gave us a word to put the net on the other side, which was Gloucester Road. Many were saved there and this is a continuing work today. It's surprising how many people want to talk into the late hours about God. Simon will always stay and evangelise them, no matter how long it takes, even in cold weather.

There are always people who need extra help such as counselling and letter writing. Also, lately we have added CLAAW which is a group of lawyer friends who help the poor in legal matters. It's going well, as Simon is able to put his legal knowledge to work.

The Street Evangelism goes on, and also we have

held Christian parties for the homeless over a few Christmases, where Simon brings the whole thing together – singers, music and great food, plus clothes for the homeless. God has always been the centre of all this outreach which comes through prayer and fasting.

I look forward to continuing this work and adding to it as God reveals what to do next. Simon has very bravely written this account of his past, which I know has been very painful for him at times. He writes with honesty and directness. He knows no other way than to be truthful and forthcoming with such powerful insights to life at the top of his society, having climbed up the ladder of success himself and then been thrown down to the bottom of that social ladder where people took full advantage of his good trusting nature. I believe he has a great ministry to these people who now have abandoned him, because what the world sees as failure God sees as success.

As someone once said, 'Cream always rises to the top.' I believe this is true of Simon. God is now gradually bringing him up, and I know that God will turn around all Simon's sorrows of the past for his benefit, and I pray *From Law to Grace* will bless all who read it Big Time.

On November 29th 2014 Simon and I launched International Child day of Prayer. We let as many as we could reach know about it, hitting America, Ireland and all over Britain. In the first year we noticed a lot going on regarding children, but 2015 more and more was being talked about in local media. We both felt God was bringing children to the forefront of our nations, their plight being brought to our attention in many parts of the world.

Nicky Cruz gave a word in Pip n Jay church that children would begin to draw their parents to Jesus; we are now hearing about this happening in the world (e.g. from Transworld radio). We both followed this vision in Bristol leading lots of youth to Christ. Simon is anointed in this work.

I urge everyone that reads Simon's book to join us in Bristol to go to your local Cathedral or Church and link with other believing Christians on 29th November 2016 to help make this and every year a great harvest as I believe God is going to let us all shake the gates of heaven for every child in this world.

Shake the gates of heaven with us now every day. Millions have already joined us; now let's push through- we are going to see a great harvest of young coming into the kingdom of God.

When you read Simon's book you are getting a great insight into one of God's apostles; signs and wonders and healings and deliverances follow his ministry. I hope to see him invited into Christian gatherings and churches with the apostolic message all over the globe for such a time as this.

*Bridget*

Last month Bridget wrote to the Queen, and she immediately wrote back supporting a National Day of Prayer, saying she only takes instructions from her ministers. She asked Bridget to contact the Prime Minister David Cameron to tell him to advise Her Majesty on this issue.

# Epilogue

Bridget and I co-ran a drop-in for the homeless for over four years, and eighteen men and women were baptised. We then went to the streets and were led by God to College Green in Bristol where we evangelised teenagers every Saturday for three years. Over one thousand were saved (which may be seen in our earliest YouTube videos). God started a revival which still continues. We have been to Yate, Bath, Keynsham and other towns in the Bristol area, as well as visiting burger bars and skate parks. Many people have been saved immediately.

Tony Gosling very kindly invited us to speak on his radio show, Bristol Community 93.2 FM, where we have done about twelve interviews so far. We have also spoken on Premier Radio. Several newspapers have featured the revival, and some cuttings are in this book.

Bridget and I have set up *CLAAW – Christian Legal Advice & Action to Win*. We have a group of lawyers on board and we act pro bono (without charge) for anyone, and have already helped quite a few people. We have one hundred percent success so far.

All this comes under the umbrella of the Bristol Underground Church, which Bridget and I set up. We have already held three big meetings at Christmas for everyone – and that especially includes the homeless. There is, as is Scriptural, an open mic (*1 Corinthians 14:26*). One guy got saved at the first one, and these meetings are also on YouTube.

Lately, there has been much success on Facebook, where I teach the Bible. We raised money for a Haitian orphanage, and have sent, and arranged to be sent from partner organisations we know all over the world, tens of thousands of Bibles, Gospels and tracts. These have gone to churches and ministries in countries including Africa, Pakistan and India.

Bridget and I have also conducted missions to Ireland, Guildford, the Isle of Wight and Bridgend in South Wales, amongst other places, and people get saved in large numbers. We have revival.

There are 150 YouTube videos under: Simonbridget. My Facebook is: Simon Alexander Farris. Our email is: bristolundergroundchurch@yahoo.co.uk and our phone number is 07984 727051.

*We are available to speak anytime, anywhere.* Bridget and I work under the prophetic and apostolic respectively and have ministered together for years, and we have found a special healing for emotions. So far I have spoken at Trinity Tabernacle where Andy Paget interviewed me for about 45 minutes about this book and my testimony. Very enjoyable. Ben Daniels, a good friend, blew the shofar and prophesied. I am looking for more opportunities, and have recently have been granted a slot to speak at Andy Paget's church.

The Scripture we use is Romans 10:13: *'Whosoever shall call on the Name of the Lord shall be saved'*, which in modern parlance means: If you ask Jesus for a place in heaven you will receive it.

Baptising Teresa Smith
in 2015

*Bridget White has written a really good prophetic poetry book called* Hands Across the Ocean, *available from online booksellers and eBay. The poems detail Bridget's poverty-stricken Irish childhood, and there are some great poems on Jesus, as well as on current events.*

*Fourteen of these poems have been turned to music. The album,* Tiny Feet, *is available for download on the CD Baby website. Copies of the book and the CD may also be obtained directly from us. The proceeds are for* Child Aid *and* Safeside, *organisations in Bristol which Bridget and I have set up to help people who have been abused.*

*I recommend both. The poetry shows Bridget's love for Jesus, and the album is really brilliant. Bridget is planning to write her eagerly awaited full life story called* The Shirtwhites's Daughter *soon.*

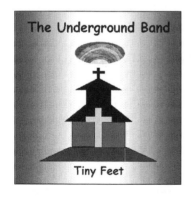

Bridget White's CD album and poetry book

We found our musician by a miracle. We were searching for composers on the internet, and I could not find any, having tried the most famous ones. I then decided to type Graham Kendrick into Facebook, and a man from Bournemouth replied, who was also called Graham Kendrick. He said, 'I suppose you're looking for the famous one, but I am also a worship leader and can I be of help?' The rest is history. Graham has produced *Tiny Feet* having worked really hard – all for free. We are immensely grateful to you, Graham, and look forward perhaps to our second album.

Robert White, Bridget's younger brother, has recorded *In the Name of Jesus, We Have the Victory* on our YouTube site *Simonbridget* and has had over 30,000 views. Thank you, Robert, and we look forward to continuing to work with you.

Bridget would like to emphasise the importance of Christians spreading the gospel. For example, I gave a leaflet in the street to a black man called Paul. A week later I saw him again and he told me that because of the leaflet he had refrained from committing suicide, and then went to a church. He is now a regular attender and has been baptised. We feel it is important to identify your Holy Spirit gift and walk in it. Bridget and I stress thus the value of Christians carrying tracts and giving them out at every opportunity.

I have learnt that nowadays people do not really bother to stand and listen to street preachers shouting at them, but in today's age where we are all educated to read, people, I think, warm to a good Christian leaflet that they can take home and digest at their leisure. I know the Bible says, 'The work of the Lord is never in vain', but obviously there are better and worser ways of doing it.

On 29th November 2014 we launched *The International Child Day of Prayer*, informing over 100 Christian ministries on Facebook, and judging from the responses and the numbers of members in each of the ministries, we believe millions may have prayed. Certainly we felt a spiritual difference in the climate that day, and after.

# Delvin native talks about finding peace in life

**OLGA AUGHEY**

From the Westmeath Examiner Saturday August 29, 2015

DELVIN native Bridget White was retracing her steps last week, visiting the places of her childhood, such as Caddagh, where she was born.

"We're just trying to acclimatise to how busy Mullingar is, it's such a busy town now," remarks Bridget. "We were in the bog yesterday so I had a good sleep last night," she laughs.

The last time Bridget returned home was three years ago. She has since released her first book, Hands Across The Ocean, a story of faith which is reflected in her poetry. She has

also produced an album called Tiny Feet. All the proceeds from the book and album sales go to helping the needy.

Bridget and colleague Simon Farris work with the poor and disadvantaged in Bristol with Bristol Underground Church. They returned to Mullingar last week for a Revival Ireland meeting, running a street church, and a meeting in the Greville Arms, where they dealt with the many issues facing people today.

Simon, a Cambridge graduate, has also written a book, Law to Grace, which details his trials in life, and how what he claims are a series of miracles

led him to lead a better and more fulfilling life.

"I had a happy childhood until I entered secondary school where I was badly bullied," says Simon.

He entered Cambridge University to study Law, and while on a gap year to Thailand, he reports that he was sexually assaulted by another male. This started a downward spiral for him.

"I was unhappy for the first time in my life. This led me to ask myself what I wanted to do with my life and I repented. I cleaned up my life because God came into my life. He started a massive succession

of miracles. I knew I wanted to spread the word of the Gospel and that's what I've been doing with my life ever since."

Bridget and Simon have been working together for 14 years, running a shelter for the homeless, and since then have helped many find peace from addiction problems, mental illness, and the trauma of abuse.

"We visit mental hospitals and prisons and we try and get our books in there to give people some hope," explains Bridget. "We want people to know that no matter how hard things seem, there is always hope.

"The songs on my album are from my poetry. One of my poems, All Is Well, was chosen in London out of 70,000 others, to go into two books. I dedicated that to my late niece Sarah. The poem seems to have a life of its own and it has helped so many.

"The key is to keep seeking help. Keep talking, through counselling or psychotherapy, keep battling, and eventually you will get better," adds Bridget, who is scarred by a difficult childhood, and is currently writing her life story.

"You have to trust that you haven't got a hopeless end, but an endless hope," she adds.

Simon Farris and Delvin native Bridget White in Mullingar last week.

In August 2015 we conducted a mission to Co Westmeath, Ireland, for ten days. We had a word that Revival Ireland was coming, and this was confirmed by a Catholic priest we met, who was one of Bridget's distant cousins.

When we gave out the tracts in Ireland, I found the best take-up rate of anywhere I've evangelised in twenty years. About six out of ten would take leaflets, and I put this down to the working of grace through the faith in Jesus that has been provided for them by the Catholic Church. We visited St Loman's Mental Hospital in Mullingar, and I gave a word at the Mullingar Christian Fellowship.

Many people took Bridget's and my books, her CD, and Chris Wright's four small books, *So, What is a Christian?; Starting Out; Help!;* and *Running Through the Bible.* (These four books are available from major online sellers as paperbacks and e-Books.)

Amongst those saved on that trip include Bridget's Aunt Nancy who is in a home with Alzheimer's. Bridget was understandably delighted to be able to help bring this about. This reminds me of an occasion about three years ago when Bridget and I went up to see my Great Aunt Winifred who had just been placed in a home after a stroke, aged ninety-six. She was barely able to communicate, but could not keep her eyes off Bridget.

Bridget led her to ask Jesus for a place in heaven, word by word. Bridget would say one word, and then Winifred would repeat it. After that, the three of us sang some old Protestant hymns together. Winifred was beaming, and we took her outside in her wheelchair where she picked some snowdrops.

Here is a poem by Bridget, from her book *Hands Across the Ocean.*

## Such Love From On High

Worldly love will come and go
As surely as the oceans waters flow;
It will have its ups and downs,
Turn you up and twist you all around.
This love is not very strong
And more often it doesn't last very long;
It takes you to a height
And then drops you like a deflated kite.

But the love I have just for you
Is gently meekly flowing true,
As naturally as the oceans waters do.
It comes down from on high;
It's truthful and without a lie,
It cares for you when you are here or there,
It always remembers and never forgets
And nothing, in return, it expects;
It lasts for ever and a day,
Whether here or there.
It watches you from afar and near,
It's without jealousy or fear;
It sees your inner hurt and pain
And wants to comfort you time and time again.
It sees your inner conflict and emotions
That are so deep; deep as the oceans
Where an earthly love cannot reach
And only love from on high can teach.

Where did I find such love just for you,
That is so humble and true?

It's a gift from God, not for me, but for you,
And in return you would see His love just for you.

Bridget White

* * *

*A word for Christians: We should share our faith with everyone we meet, at all times.*

*A word from Prophetess Bridget. John 15: Abide in Jesus and you will bear much fruit. The word is to empower you to realise that you can bear much fruit based upon your relationship with Jesus. So go and make disciples. Be encouraged – if we can do it, so can you.*

*Please feel free to photocopy the tract overleaf and add your own contact details.*

# Heaven

GLOBAL WARMING could destroy the world, but Jesus is coming back and will put everything right again.

So what sort of life should you live? One that pleases Him, because although He came the first time to save people, He is coming the second time to judge.

There is a marvellous promise in the Bible that whoever asks Jesus for a place in heaven will receive it. So go on, do that now. Pray, 'Please, Jesus, give me a place in heaven. Amen.'

Repent. The Bible says the acts of the sinful nature include: 'Sexual immorality, impurity and lewdness, idolatry and witchcraft, hatred, contentions, jealousy, fits of rage, selfish ambition, divisions, heresies and envy, drunkenness and revelry etc.' Also, 'Evil thoughts, murders, thefts, false witness and blasphemies, pride, greed and folly.'

Instead, follow Jesus. He commands us all to spread the gospel. Be baptised (fully under water – not infant christening). Persevere to death and you will go to heaven with an everlasting reward for every good deed you have done. Amen.

17065968R00077

Printed in Poland
by Amazon Fulfillment
Poland Sp. z o.o., Wrocław